"Affable and Humane"

The history of the development and growth of Methodism in the King's Lynn Circuit, from the coming of John Wesley in 1771.

W.F. Sampson,
Clenchwarton,
King's Lynn.

May, 1998

ACKNOWLEDGEMENTS

The author would like to say thank you, to all the members of the Lynn Circuit who have provided information and photographs, also to

Reverend Barbara Savage,
Reverend Colin D Harbach,
Reverend John Garfoot,
Brian Hart, Lynn Circuit Archivist,
Dr E.D Graham, Connexional Archives Liaison Officer,
Bryan Tolhurst, The Methodist Church, London,
The Staff of Lynn Library,
The Editor of the Lynn News,
A & C Black (Publishers) (EP Publishing),
The Wesley Historical Society, East Anglia District,
Mike Brown, for computer expertise,
my son Grahame, for editing,
Rhona Morris, for reading the final draft, and finally,
my wife Joyce, for her wholehearted support and incredible patience.

W.F Sampson. 1998.

Printed by Clanpress of King's Lynn.

ISBN 0 9522132 1 4

CONTENTS

PAGE

LIST OF ILLUSTRATIONS

PAGE

FOREWORD

I suppose that, over the past two centuries, many books and articles have been written about John Wesley, about his evangelistic zeal for Jesus Christ and that Gospel to be spread abroad.

But John Wesley lived at a time of great social change in our land.

There are many, indeed, who would testify that his Christian fervour deflected what could have been an English "French Revolution."

And so it is, I believe, that any book about Wesley that seeks to give a balanced view - and any book about the people called "Methodists" - need to have that fine balance. On the one hand, to show clearly that Wesley - and the Methodist people who followed on after him - see the importance of a personal relationship with Jesus as paramount, together with Scriptural holiness; but on the other hand that measure of care, consideration and concern for the social aspects of the world in which all of us exist.

It is with these things in mind that I commend this book to you.

Its conception was during a time of searching and contemplation by Bill.

Its gestation has, I know, called for him to spend many hours researching and turning up old records.

Its birth, I believe, will be joyful - for it will achieve what Bill set out to do; to take a good hard look at why the Methodist Church is here, in this small area of Norfolk, in the closing years of this century.

Barbara Savage.

15, Churchgateway,
Terrington St. Clement,
King's Lynn, Norfolk.

July, 1997

INTRODUCTION

In the main, this account is largely based on original records, including those from Circuit Minute Books. My sources are listed in appendix I; there are of course, gaps where records are missing. Quotations from the actual minutes are included and these are in italics; the original spelling has been preserved in order to maintain the atmosphere of the period.

Included in the text is information on 56 Societies that have been part of the King's Lynn Wesleyan and Primitive Methodist Circuits during the past one hundred and fifty years, and of which thirteen remain. Wesleyan sources are scarce and other Methodists, such as the New Connexion, have no primary sources available, so the majority of the story is based on the Primitive Methodists, and oh, what a story!

It is a source of wonder that a small number of people, having little to offer but faith, could, despite all the odds against them, inspire and plan the building of Chapels and schoolrooms, especially during the nineteenth century.

It is not the purpose of this book to highlight the differences between the Wesleyans and Primitive Methodists, but the Primitives were mainly poor people. According to Armes(1) ***"They were noisy, but devoted. They were harmless and interfered with no man, but if possible, to do him good."*** They had little formal education, many could not read or write, but several were to achieve fame as Local Preachers. For example, James Rasberry of Gayton, left school at the age of seven in 1862. He was to become a Sunday School teacher, superintendent, secretary, Local Preacher and an Evangelist,and, quoting from his story(2), ***"Walking from twenty to thirty miles on a Sunday to preach the Gospel."***

Notes:-
(1)Memories of Lynn: William Armes 1858. Published in the Lynn Advertiser 1872 following his death the same year.
(2)Life of James Rasberry of Gayton. 1927. (Circuit Archives).

Chapter one

THE COMING OF JOHN WESLEY

On Wednesday 6th November 1771, the Reverend John Wesley made the first of twelve visits to Lynn Regis. He had preached at Bury the previous evening and rode to Lynn on horseback through heavy rain.

John Wesley was nearly 69 and had been preaching for 46 years. As an itinerant Anglican Priest, he had travelled widely spreading the Gospel. He had often visited Norwich and had passed close to Lynn a few years earlier, when travelling from Norwich to the Fens. Why visit Lynn now?

The answer lay with a Mr and Mrs Crawford who lived in Tower Street, Lynn. They had been converted by John Wesley and his brother Charles, when living at Newcastle on Tyne. The Crawfords were of humble stock and concerned for the moral and spiritual welfare of Lynn's citizens(1). They asked John Wesley to send his disciples and opened their house to travelling preachers from Norwich. Then John Wesley arrived. He recorded that *"the people received the word with joy, though few, as yet, had any root in themselves."*

The following day, John Wesley was informed that the prisoners in the gaol would like religious counselling, although his visit is unrecorded in the Hall Book(2). He noted that they listened *"with the utmost eagerness" and went on to say "who knows but one or two may retain it?"*

In the evening Wesley again preached at the house of the Crawfords. There was insufficient room for all who wished to hear him. He noted that *"those who could not get in, were noisy at first; but in a while they went quietly away."* There had been mob violence in other places.

During this first visit to Lynn, John Wesley took stock of the town and its citizens and made favourable comments, likening some of the houses to *"little palaces."* Impressed by the Tuesday Market Place he considered it *"a spacious and noble square more beautiful than either that at Yarmouth or Norwich."* The townsfolk he described as *"affable and humane. They have the openess and frankness common throughout the country, and they add to it good nature and courtesy."*

John Wesley rode to Norwich the next day, and did not return for almost two years. Eventually, on Monday 1st November 1773, he set out from London for Norfolk and came to Lynn to find members of the infant Society. He was horrified to learn they had been *"torn to pieces."* Some of them having been converted to Calvinism.

Wesley wrote that he *"did all he could to heal the breach, both in public and private; and having recovered a few, I left them all in peace, and went to Norwich on Wednesday."*

On Tuesday 5th December 1775, he travelled from Norwich arriving at Lynn in the afternoon. In the evening he preached in what he referred to as *"the new house*(3)." He noted that it *"would hardly contain one half of the congregation; and those that could not get in were tolerably patient, considering they could hear but a few words."*

At 1am the next morning Wesley was asked to visit a sick man who thought himself to be dying. Wesley reported that the power of prayer was so powerful that the man sat up in bed and shouted *"I shall not die but live."*

During the day Wesley visited many of those who had remained loyal to his doctrine plus those who had left the Society having been converted to Calvinism. In the evening he noted that the Chapel was *"quite too small and yet even those who could not get in were silent; a circumstance which I have seldom observed in any other part of England."*

Some of his visits to Lynn were fleeting ones and Wesley made no observations on these except to comment on the travel arrangements. For example, on Thursday 20th November 1777, after preaching at Norwich, at 5, he left for Lynn the same day and on Saturday 22nd, he took a chaise soon after 12 and reached London in the afternoon.

Two years later, on Monday 1st November 1779, he was back in Lynn to *"settle the little affairs there."* He left for Colchester on the Wednesday.

Earlier in 1776, King's Lynn formed a separate Circuit instead of being part of the Norwich Circuit.

On Wednesday 31st October 1781, he left Walsingham for Lynn and preached in the evening to what he described as *"a very genteel congregation."* He wrote that *"I spoke more strongly than I am accustomed to do so, and hope they were not all sermon-proof."* On Friday 2nd November, he returned to London.

Two years later, on Wednesday 29th October 1783, Wesley came expecting trouble, but found things much better than anticipated. He referred to the behaviour of a Mr G... and found to his surprise that more good than harm had been done such that Mr G... had been judged by the congregation and found wanting. Wesley noted *"people in general cried 'let that bad man go,' they will do better without him."* He also observed that *"the house was sufficiently crowded with serious hearers."* He left for London on Saturday 1st November.

On Tuesday 25th October 1785, Wesley travelled from Lynn from Norwich and recorded that Lynn had, for a long time *"been a cold and comfortless place."* He arrived to find completely different circumstances, in that *"two young, zealous, active preachers strongly urging the people to expect a full and present salvation, have enlivened both the Society and the congregation(4)."*

After preaching, Wesley discovered that no stage coach left for London until Friday, so instead took a postchaise. He reached Downham

Market between 10 and 11pm and was advised that, because the night was so dark, it was inadvisable to travel over Ely roads, as they ran between two banks across which were many bridges where the coachman had no room for error. Wesley recorded, *"we knew in who we trusted, and pushed forward, till about one on Thursday we reached London."*

That journey highlighted some of the perils of 18th century night travel on rural Fen roads. The journey from Downham took about 26 hours. He was now 81 years old and, although in good health, had been reluctantly persuaded to travel in a stagecoach rather than on horseback.

On Tuesday 10th October 1786, mindful that he had promised to preach in *"their new house at Lynn*(3)" and with the weather good, Wesley planned to journey from London. He had ordered two places in the stagecoach due to reach Lynn on Tuesday 10th at noon. However, two places were booked in a stagecoach called the 'Diligence', which did not arrive in Lynn until between 9 and 10pm. Wesley lamented that *"by this means I lost one of three evenings, which I proposed to spend there."* He wrote *"I spent Wednesday and Thursday with much satisfaction with a very loving and lively people, increasing in grace as well as in number, and adorning the doctrine of God our Saviour."*

In the evening of Tuesday 30th September 1788, Wesley took a stagecoach from London to Lynn, arriving there about noon on Wednesday 1st October. He recorded, *"I spent all the time with much satisfaction, as I had never found them so much alive before."* He left on Friday 3rd, for Norwich, in a coach called the 'Expedition.'

The following year, on Tuesday 13th October 1789, he travelled in the night mailcoach from London to Barton Mills, transferred to a chaise and completed the journey to Lynn, arriving on Wednesday the following day. He wrote *"the heavy rain prevented tender people from attending in the evening."* This from a man who was 86 years old!

John Wesley wrote on Friday 1st January 1790, *"I am now an old man, decayed from hand to foot. My eyes are dim; my right hand shakes much; my mouth is hot and dry every morning. I have a lingering fever almost every day. My motion is weak and slow. However blessed be God, I do not slacken my labour. I can preach and write still."*

John Wesley made his last trip to Lynn, via Norwich, on Monday 18th October 1790. As no stagecoach was leaving that day he was obliged to take a postchaise. When the party reached Dereham, they had to retain the same horses as no fresh post-horses were available. At Swaffham, a congregation was awaiting him and Wesley noted *"they seemed quite willing to receive instruction."* However, as no post-horses were available he had to take a single horse chaise. Wesley gave a vivid description of the prevailing weather; *"the wind with misling rain, came full in our faces, and we had nothing to screen us from it; so that I was thoroughly chilled from head to foot."*

Wesley found that the earnestness of the Lynn congregation soon made him forget what he described as a *"little inconvenience."*

He stayed at Tower House, in Tower Place, the residence of the Vicar of St. Margaret's, the Reverend Edwards. The following evening, all the Lynn clergymen, except one who was lame, were present to hear him preach. Wesley noted that *"they are all prejudiced in favour of the Methodists, as indeed are most of the townsmen; who give a fair proof by contributing so much to our Sunday Schools, so that there is near twenty pounds in hand."* On Wednesday he left to preach at Diss, having witnessed how public opinion had swung in his favour since the early days, when he had experienced abuse and occasional violence from hostile crowds.

On Wednesday 2nd March 1791, the Reverend John Wesley died at City Road, London, in his 88th year. He had been 65 years in the Anglican Ministry and 52 years an itinerant preacher.

Notes:-

(1)History of King's Lynn: H.J Hillen. Vol.2.p.547. It is recorded that Mrs Crawford was alive in 1817, aged 103. Hillen referred to Lynn as a 'benighted town' which suggests a degree of ignorance and darkness prevailing. Lynn was renowned as an active sea and fishing port and agricultural centre with a bustling market. The Universal Directory of Trading, Commerce and Manufacturing of 1793-1798 stated:- "there are more gentry and consequently more gaiety than Yarmouth, even Norwich; here being such plenty of eatables and drinkables, that Spelman says Ceres and Bacchus seem to have established their magazines here." For seamen, farmers and residents, there was approximately one licensed premise for every hundred people in the Borough. In 1892, the King's Lynn Vigilance Committee published a map of King's Lynn showing 180 licensed premises for the 18,625 population, or put another way, one house in every 22 was licensed for the sale of intoxicating liquor! A high proportion of the "drinking shops" were in the poorer districts where, according to the Vigilance Committee, "They flourish where wives and children starve and pine."

(2)A Royal Charter of 1537 allowed the town to keep a gaol and in 1615, rooms under the Town Hall were used as cells. George III's reign continued a punitive penal system allowed by the statutes, with public hanging for a number of crimes. In 1784, Joseph Beaton was condemned to be hung by the neck, for robbery, and was executed having been sentenced at the courtroom above the gaol. In 1723, Thomas German was hanged for burglary on the gallows at the South Gates. In 1751, according to William Richards(History of King's Lynn 1812) - a man called Gafferson was hanged in chains on a gibbet upon the South Lynn common. He also recorded that in 1782, a woman named Howard was stoned in the pillory and said "we know not for what crime." (Gibbeting was not abolished until 1834; the pillory not until 1837). Between 1823 and 1827, Sir Robert Peel, as Home Secretary, abolished capital punishment for several crimes, but public hanging was not abolished until 1868. These 'relaxations' came far too late to save a brother and sister, aged 7 and 11, who were hanged in Lynn in 1708 for felony.

(3)Wesley called Chapels 'new houses.' Hillen recorded (History of King's Lynn. Vol.2.p.548) that the first Methodist Chapel was built on the South side of North Clough Lane and was in existence in 1788. This ran parallel to South Clough Lane (now replaced by a swimming pool and carpark) with an open tidal drain, the Clough Fleet, flowing between them. This may have been the Chapel referred to by John Wesley. Alternatively, it may have been the new preaching house in New Conduit Street. (William Armes-Memories of Lynn 1858- said that "John Wesley first preached in this town in a house on the south side of New Conduit Street, near the east end, The house may still be recognised by a small upper window, having a red brick arch). Methodist Ministers at this time were William Palmer,John M'Kersey and John Gaulter. Itinerant preachers were lodged in the home of a builder Mr Samuel Newham, a convert of the Crawfords. He started a Sunday School, and about 1787 built a house for the preachers and their families. The Chapel was extended into a building 42 feet long by 30 feet wide with galleries on three sides. However, this was still not of sufficient size and the building was eventually abandoned as a Chapel. Plans were then made for a much larger Chapel in Tower Street.

(4)The two young, zealous, active preachers were William Palmer and Charles Bland. According to Hall's Circuits and Ministers 1765-1896, they were Ministers in the Lynn Circuit in 1785.

Chapter two

THE GROWTH OF METHODISM

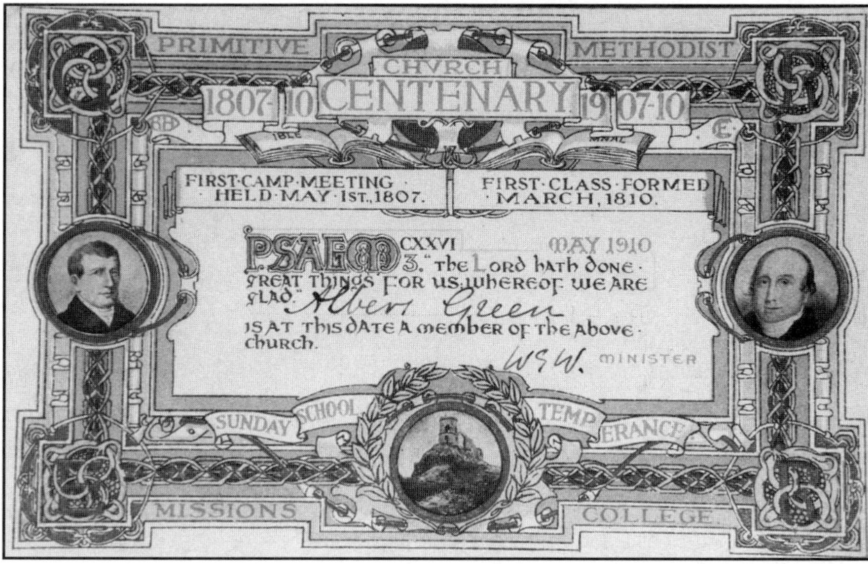

PM Centenary Members Ticket showing Hugh Bourne & William Clowes

Methodism continued to flourish in the Lynn Circuit and beyond. In 1791, a separate Circuit was formed in Wells from Lynn (Later to be called the Walsingham Circuit).

In 1797, the first Sunday School was opened in Lynn(1). Also in 1797, the Methodist New Connexion broke away from the main body(2). A day school was opened in 1812.

Another independent Circuit began in 1805 at Wisbech, from the Lynn Circuit. Methodism had started earlier in Wisbech when two Lynn preachers, Mr Ashmead and Mr Charles Kyte, were welcomed with *"showers of stones and mud*(3)." However, not all Wisbech men were against them for a Mr William Bell opened his barn for services.

In 1813, a third independent Circuit was formed from Lynn, in Swaffham.

Plans for a new Chapel in Tower Street came to fruition in 1811, when two Methodist preachers, the Reverends Bernard Slater and Thomas Pollard, bought a property site in Tower Site from George Rainer Whincup for between £800 and £900, by a conveyancing system known as lease and release(4). One of the occupiers of the site was Hart Jones, a Jewish man who operated a synagogue. In another dwelling had lived Mr and Mrs Crawford, where the first preaching place had been.

The Chapel cost £4,500 to build. It opened in 1813 and could seat 1,500 people. It was considered rather a grandiose building and was referred to rather sarcastically by William Richards as *"the splendid Methodist Minster"*(5)." The Ministers were the Reverends Maxmillian Wilson and Thomas Ludlam. It was extensively refurbished in 1884.

A secession occurred in 1807, when the Primitive Methodists were formed by Hugh Bourne and William Clowes. These two preachers were expelled from membership for conducting camp meetings in Staffordshire (the first one had been at Mow Cop). These were outdoor services of which the Wesleyan Methodists strongly disapproved. The new brotherhood reached Lynn in about 1821 (see chapter 3).

The Wesleyan almshouses, costing £1000, were built and endowed by Benjamin Smith in 1829 for eight poor women.

In 1834, another secession occurred when a nucleus of people, objecting to the autocratic nature of the Conference, formed the Wesleyan Methodist Association(6).

A Conference decision in 1849 resulted in a further secession. This new body was called the Wesleyan Reform Association(7).

The Wesleyan Building Programme in Lynn continued when a

Chapel at North End was built in 1862(8). This was eventually sold to the Primitive Methodists and a new Chapel built in Pilot Street, which had 400 sittings. In 1888, a Chapel was built at the junction of South Everard Street and London Road. The architect was Mr J.A Hillam and the builders Messrs Leech and Allflatt. Cost was £2,500.

The Tower Street Chapel installed an organ in 1852 for £200, built by Nicholsons of Rochdale. In 1876, a new organ was installed by Costloe and Sons of Isleworth.

The Lynn Wesleyan Extension Scheme was proposed in 1882 and entailed raising £6,000 towards building and renovating Sunday School accommodation.

For several years limited space had seriously affected the three schools, at Tower Street, North End and London Road; each of them having more children than could comfortably be accommodated. (There were 800 scholars and teachers). A site, opposite the Tower Street Chapel was offered to the Trustees by Mr Josiah Carver, which they secured and commenced the building of a large room with six separate classrooms and other facilities. At North End, adjoining property to the existing Chapel was offered. After purchase, the previous accommodation was doubled.

London Road was felt to be a special case, having more children applying for admission than could be received. A suitable site was eventually secured.

Tower Street was allocated £3,300 (purchase and building school, renovation of Chapel), London Road £2,000 and North End £700. Superintendent Minister was Rev. W Malpass, treasurer J Jackson, secretary Robert Whiteman. The Committee was:- Messrs Alfred Jermyn, William Thompson, W.L Armes, C.H Lemon, J Paul, F.A Curson and F Ollett.

The 1887 Circuit Plan showed that, in addition to the three Chapels in Lynn, there were thirteen Chapels in the surrounding district, eg. Gaywood, Terrington St.Clement, Tilney All Saints, St.Germans, Saddlebow, Watlington, Grimston, Gayton, West Lynn, Blackborough, West Winch, Pentney and Narborough.

Ministers were the Revs. Wm Edward Gardner and J Hawkins Pawlyn. The Circuit Officers included:- Mr Alfred Jermyn and Mr J Paul (Circuit Stewards), Mr C Allen (Sunday School secretary), and Mr J.W Groom (Temperance secretary).There were also 33 Local Preachers, 25 of them living in Lynn. A note on the plan said *"no candidate can be fully admitted as a Local Preacher until he has read the standard sermons of Mr Wesley and his notes on the New Testament."* Tower Street and Terrington Churches were registered for the solemnization of marriage.

The Class System developed by John Wesley, resulted from the conversion of many people throughout the Country. He formed them into classes, with leaders. Each member paid a quarterly subscription and received a membership ticket. The 1887 plan showed that this practice was continuing with 27 Class Leaders in Lynn (3 were junior Class Leaders) and 11 in Terrington. A Notice said *"the Society Stewards will kindly have pulpit announcements made of the renewal of 'tickets.' The leaders are expected to do their utmost to secure a good attendance."* The two Ministers made quarterly visitations of the classes.

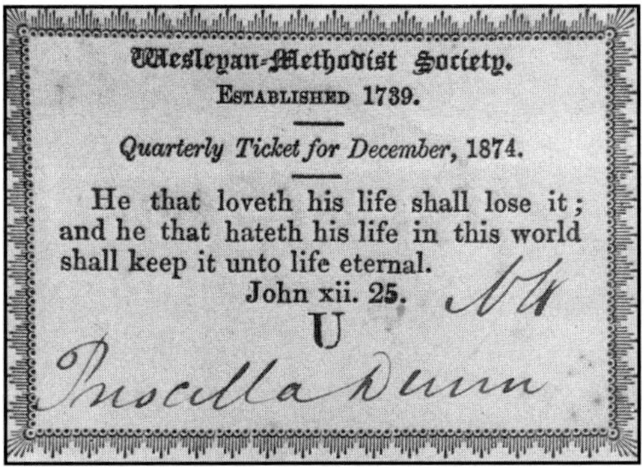

Quarterly Membership Ticket Dec.1874.

Wesleyan Cottage Services were also held(9).

The Stranger's Friend Society was established late in the 18th century by members of the Wesleyan Methodist Society and congregation, with a view to helping poor families cope with hunger and disease(10). Locally, Mr Samuel Newham was treasurer and Mr James Burch secretary. In Lynn the annual report from 1807-1808 showed that

WESLEYAN COTTAGE SERVICES.

"Go Work in my Vineyard." **KINGS LYNN, 1886—7.** "The Love of Christ constraineth us."

MEETING PLACES.	TIME.	DEC. 12	19	26	JANUARY. 2	9	16	23	30	FEBRUARY. 6	13	20	27	MCH 6
The Lifeboat, North End ...	Tu. 8 0	2	3	4	5	6	1	2	3	4	5	6	1	2
Union Lane Mission Room...	W. 8 0	3	4	5	6	1	2	3	4	5	6	1	2	3
All Saints' Street Mission Room	M. 8 0	4	5	6	1	2	3	4	5	6	1	2	3	4
Atto's Yard, Norfolk Street. ...	F. 8 0	5	6	1	2	3	4	5	6	1	2	3	4	5
Edward Street, Mrs. Hides	W. 8 0	6	1	2	3	4	5	6	1	2	3	4	5	6
All Saints' Street Mission Room	Th. 8 0	1	2	3	4	5	6	1	2	3	4	5	6	1

NAMES IN COMPANIES

1 Ranshawe, *(Leader)*, R. Bush, J. Frost, Bonn, Franklin, Fisher, Hendry, Lusher, Pye, Mrs. Foreman, Mrs. Neville, Mrs. Howard, Mrs. Green, Mrs. Addison and Mrs. Pye.

2 Rands, *(Leader)*, Bush, Atkins, B. Fox, Burman, Howes, J. Emmerson, Johnson, Ashbey, T. Wildbur, Darby, Gunn, Rason, Mrs. Nelson, Mrs. Boswell, Mrs. Woods, Mrs. Rason and Miss Bower

3 Creak, *(Leader)*, Eggett, Jermyn, Mitchell, W. Thompson, Capt. Smith, Foreman, Gham, H. Triance, Dawes, Kirk, J. Whiley, Whitehead, Mrs S. Smith, Mrs Haythorpe, Mrs. Jones, Mrs. Williman, Mrs. Whitehead

4 Allflatt, *(Leader)*, King, Burman, senr., E. Catton, Jno. Catton, W. Catton, Ping, Mrs. R. Wildbur, Mrs. King, Mrs. Woollard, Mrs. Allflatt, Mrs. Whiley, Mrs. Catton, Misses Colman, Pearson and Gamble.

5 Burton, *(Leader)*, Gibson, Bradbrook, G. Thompson, Ashley, Triance, Whitmore, Hides, Howell, Mrs. Fisher, Mrs. Waters, Mrs. Burton, Mrs. Walker, Mrs. H. Frost, and Miss Gilbert.

6 Wright, *(Leader)*, Scott, Paul, F. A. Curson, Frost, Hall, Hides, Lily, Harkness, Mrs. Paul, Mrs. Groom, Mrs. Hall, Mrs. Fysh, Mrs. Twiss, Misses Cozens, Smith and Docking

Wesleyan Cottage Services Plan 1886-87

subscriptions were £75.13.1d of which £75.4.6d had been distributed among 189 families in 846 visits.

Smith's Charity was another benevolent charity which operated from Tower Street Chapel in 1881(11). The £18 annual income from pew rents was distributed to poor members in coal and money.

The 1918 Plan showed the same sixteen Chapels with the addition of Union Lane listed as a Place of Worship. This was a small Mission building located in what, by 1996, was the staff carpark of Messrs Debenhams.

Methodist Union occurred in 1932. The Wesleyan, Primitive and United Methodists, joined together nationally to form the Methodist Church.

The 1932 Plan gave the following special notices,eg. *"On July 31st there will be general interchange of pulpits among the three Methodist Churches in Lynn and*

District. On September 20th to 25th, the United Conference of the three Methodist Churches meets in London. On September 28th the United District Synod will meet at Norwich. Some of the United Conference Meetings will be broadcast and it is hoped to arrange for reception in Tower Street Chapel. In view of these special happening we invite you to spend much time in prayer for God's blessing upon them, and we ask that special prayer meetings be arranged in our Chapels on September 20th, the day of the Uniting Conference."

Notes:-

(1)The History of King's Lynn:H.J Hillen. Vol. 2.p.549.

(2)Ibid. Vol.2. p.646, This was a secession from the Wesleyan Methodists by members who were unhappy with matters regarding discipline and Church government over which they felt they had no voice. Leader was the Rev. Alexander Kilham. A Chapel was built in Lynn in 1853, called the Tabernacle.In 1868, there were three Ministers in the Lynn New Connexion Circuit, one of whom was the Rev. George Hallatt, one of the prime figures in the temperance movement. The Tabernacle was succeeded by the Trinity Church, which was built on the site of the old Tabernacle at a cost of £1,300. The architect was Mr A.H Goodall of Nottingham, who employed the Early English style. A schoolroom and Minister's office were built at the same time as the Chapel. The Reverend H.T Marshall D.D. of Ashton performed the opening ceremony on 2nd December, 1891. There is very little information on Chapels in the Circuit. New Connexional Chapels were built in Clenchwarton and Terrington St.Clement. The Chapel in Clenchwarton became a private dwelling in the 1930's.

(3)Wesley Historical Society Publication No.66. East Anglia District.

(4)This was an early method of avoiding the payment of tax when property was sold. The seller would arrange to lease the property for a short period to the buyer for a minuscule amount. The release documents would then be drawn up and issued. In the sale of the Tower Street property, the lease documents were issued on 28th November 1811 and the release documents were drawn up and issued the following day.

(5)History of Lynn: William Richards MA. 1812.

(6)The History of King's Lynn:H.J Hillen. Vol.2. p.647/648. Hillen noted that little was known of the movement, but in four years they had developed into a small Circuit of 5 Local Preachers, 23 members and 25 Sunday School scholars. The Society were assisted by the Baptists. It is believed that a Chapel was opened in North Clough Lane in 1843. Hillen said that the zenith of prosperity was reached in 1849, when the Society numbered 113 members, 2 Chapels and 3 preaching places.

(7)Ibid. Vol.2. p.648/649. A Chapel was built in Lynn, on the west side of London Road and became the All Saints Missions Room. Chapels were also erected at other villages, including Gayton and Grimston. In 1850 the Chapel at Highgate was consecrated for worship, which the Society rented from George Cozens. (it was sold to the Primitive Methodists in 1852). A much larger Chapel was built in Railway Road. It was designed by Cruso and Maberley and built by Bennett and Rolin for a tender of £1,210 in 1853. The overall cost was about £2,000. It could accommodate 800 people.

The Wesleyan Reformers later amalgamated with the Methodist New Connexion. This resulted in the building of the Trinity Church on the site of the old Tabernacle. Later, this body would join with the Wesleyan Associates to form the Methodist Free Church.

(8)Ibid. Vol.2. p.549.

(9)Wesleyan Cottage Service Plan 1886-87. Services were held at the Lifeboat (North End), Union Lane Mission Room, All Saint's Street Mission Room, Atto's Yard in Norfolk Street and Mrs Hide's, (Edward Street). Members were divided into six companies and met weekly, rotating round the meeting places.

(10)A preliminary enquiry into the sewage, drainage and supply of water and the sanitary condition of the inhabitants of the Borough of King's Lynn was made in 1853 by William Lee Esq,CE, Superintending Inspector. The key statistic that had resulted in the enquiry was that "The annual rates of mortality for the last seven years have greatly exceeded the proportion of 23 to 1,000 of the population of the Borough."

Among the witnesses to the enquiry was an inhabitant, Mr Joseph Hodgkinson, whose testimony included:- "I reside in Wood Street. There are privies at the West End of the street, one to five houses. There is a great number of cow sheds, and when the cows are removed in summer, the places are generally stocked with pigs. The excrement and the evaporation is very noxious, and many of the neighbours, including my own family, are frequently troubled with diarrhoea in consequence. There may be 300 to 400 inhabitants here."

A letter was read from a Dr Hamilton dated 1790. A precis of which is:- "Lynn is intersected by several fresh water creeks called here fleets, which empty themselves into the river, besides which there are several drains or common sewers, which empty themselves into those creeks. As the creeks take the tides and the ground is low lying, parts of the town are liable to flooding. Many of the ground floors of houses, instead of being raised above the problem, descend a step or two below the surface and as it were invite the mischief."

Another, Dr Whiting gave evidence and said "That when he arrived in Lynn in 1823 he found many of the evils of 1790 still existing. In 1826 a most severe epidemic raged, corresponding in almost all respects with those in 1779, 1780 and 1781. The remitting fever was universally epidemic, more violent, more frequently fatal, and spread through families, villages and towns subsequent to 1826. Intermittent and their sequelae, diseased liver, dropsy, and etc. were frequent and severe. Particularly among the labouring population but not confined to them."

Statistics showed that from 1841-1851, there was an average of 431 deaths a year out of an average population of 17,503. This gave a mortality rate of 24.5 persons per 1,000 of the population. (In 1841, 61 registration districts in England and Wales recorded 16.01 deaths per 1,000 of the population).

Mr Lee stated "In eleven years within the Borough amount to the awful number of 1643 deaths in excess." The proportion of deaths to births is almost twice as great in Lynn as it is in the other registration districts. It is apparent that a large proportion of births "is only born to die."

(11)Statement of the accounts called Smith's Charity. 31.12.1881.

Chapter three

THE PRIMITIVE METHODISTS

The Primitive Methodists came to mission Lynn when John Oscroft and Edward Wildbur were sent from the Nottingham Circuit. It is believed that they held their first open-air service outside the South Gates.

Rev. John Oscroft

However, maintaining the Primitive Methodist tradition of seeking out the poorer areas, they moved to North End and preached to a congregation in a sail maker's loft in Bennet's Yard, Black Goose Street (now St. Nicholas Street).

By 1822, Primitive Methodism had grown to encompass 57 preaching places in the Lynn area and a plan was printed. In the same year, a division occurred when one of the Ministers took 70 members away to form an alternative Society; they met in a room in Coronation Square, Lynn. What was left of a weakened movement was strengthened by the arrival of Messrs Charlton and Whitby from Nottingham. Many more people were converted and new Societies formed, so that in 1824, Lynn became a separate Circuit (No.159) in the Norwich District. Another division occurred which was cured by the healing influence of the Rev.W.G Bellham who began his first Ministry at Lynn in 1825.

Bennet's Yard

The First Chapel in London Road was built in 1826. It was a leasehold Chapel subject to a ground rent of £5.10.0 per annum (payable to Mr Ayre of Rising). The Rev.Bellham encouraged the children to collect farthings in fund raising. This 'farthing mania' covered the whole Circuit. One village was so thoroughly canvassed that it was said *"there was not one farthing to be found in the place"*, and *"one little girl went a distance of three miles to exchange a penny for four farthings."* The Chapel was a plain building. The interior was lit by candlelight and many of the seats were backless forms.

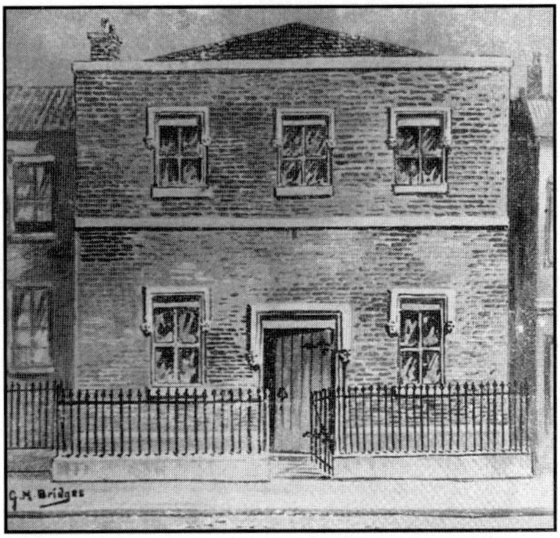

The first P.M Chapel

Missioning was undertaken with vigour. In 1832, Lynn sent James Pole to mission Docking,(this was made a separate Circuit in 1844). In 1834, the Rev. W Kirby was sent to mission Peterborough (on foot). His efforts were so successful, that Peterborough formed a separate Circuit in 1840, with 140 members.

The Class Structure started by John Wesley continued with meetings at Chapels, schoolrooms and houses at different days of the week. In 1838, Lynn had ten classes:-

(1)Friday night Class,(37 members + 13 on trial) led by the Travelling Preacher met in the schoolroom.
(2)Sunday Afternoon Class, (22 members + 8 on trial) led by Martha Gittens, met in the schoolroom after preaching.
(3)Thursday Night Class, (29 members + 8 on trial) Leader Thomas Cork, A/Leader Arthur Sainty, met in the schoolroom.
(4)North End Class, (6 members + 9 on trial)led by Cathrine Cushing.
(5)Brother Cooper's Class, (13 members + 4 on trial) led by William Cooper, A/Leader William Rounce, met in Red Cow St.(now Church St.)
(6)Monday Night Class, (44 members + 26 on trial) led by Martha Morris, met in Norfolk Street.

(7)Sunday Morning Class, (15 members + 3 on trial) led by James Sheldrick and met in Brother Sheldrick's house.
(8)Monday Night Class, (10 members)led by William Cooper, met at Sister Bell's house.
(9)Brother Smith's Class, (8 members) led by John Smith, met in Norfolk Street.
(9)Monday Night Class, (33 members) led by Hannah Bone, met in the Schoolroom.

The Preachers' Plan for 1844-45, showed that there were 32 preaching places and Revival meetings were planned at 19 of them. Listed were 71 preachers (plus three on trial and three Exhorters). Brother A Sainty was Circuit Steward and Brother W Lift, secretary. The Circuit Committee consisted of Brothers Cooper, Sheldrick, Rounce, Bottom, Guymer, Merry, Salmon, Reynolds, White, Coe and Lincoln.

In 1846 there were 30 places on the Plan. West Lynn and Setch were left off. The additions were St.Mary's(which was to be remissioned) and Tilney High End. Revival meetings were planned at eleven places. Camp Meetings were planned at Tilney High End, Gayton, Fincham and Clenchwarton. Trouble may have occurred because five years later the Committee agreed *"that two policemen be sought for the purpose of protecting the camp meetings."*

Of Circuits, travel and wages. The dictionary defines 'circuit' as the act of moving round. This specifies the Travelling Preachers role. They walked from place to place until horse transport, bicycles, trains or cars became available to them.

In the early days, preachers had barely enough to live on (but neither did the agricultural labourer in Norfolk). In 1822 the rule was that single men were to be paid a salary not exceeding £4 a quarter, and they were not allowed to bring in any bill or bills either for meat, drink, washing, lodging or medical aid of any kind. Married men were to be paid a sum not exceeding 14/- per week with the same conditions applying regarding bills, etc. Gibbard wrote *"no wonder they were all teetotallers!."*

The Conference Regulations prohibited Circuits from running into debt "*whether preachers have or have not their salaries.*" It is evident that on occasions they did not, for example, the 1847 Quarterly Circuit Committee minutes of 14th June, stated "*that the travelling preachers be allowed to make a collection in every place to make up their salaries.*" The same meeting passed the following resolution, "*that we write to the General Council to offer them a preacher should they have an opening for one, as our financial position is such that we cannot meet the increase of expenditure.*"

The Quarterly Meeting of 14th December 1847, recorded "*that there be some New Year's collecting cards printed towards making up the deficit of the preacher's salaries.*" On 19th June 1848, it was decided to write to one of the Ministers, as follows:- "*that a letter be sent to Bro Ward informing him of the financial state of the Circuit and recommending him to the consideration thereof of thinking it would be to the benefit of the Circuit and more to his benefit if he see an opening to embrace it as we shall not be able to pay anything like the 14/- salary.*"

There was an improvement by the 16th September 1851, for example, "*that the deficient salaries be paid to the preachers being £7.14.11d each viz. Bros Langham and Johnson. That this meeting make payments of the whole of Mr Ward's money. That the friends who have pledged themselves to raise the whole of Mr Ward's money have liberty to beg of their friends up to the time the rule allows. That should the effort be not successful to get the amount, the offer of Mr Lincoln be accepted to lend the amount required and that repaid it be. The effort not allowed to infringe any preachers efforts.*"

It was obviously more expensive for the Circuit to support a married Minister, especially with children, than for a single Minister, thus periodic applications, up to 1915, were made to the District Meeting and Conference "*to obtain relief from a third Married Minister.*"

The Circuit Committee gave approval or sat in judgement on everything connected with the Circuit. Permission was given for camp and revival meetings, various anniversaries as well as approval for building and cleaning Chapels. They also expected the Superintendent Minister to be a man of all talents, ie, a Preacher of the Gospel with ability to discuss plans and specifications with architects and builders, handle correspondence, keep and review accounts, draw up documents, settle disputes, etc, etc.

Disciplinary matters included activities the Circuit Steward thought were likely to bring the Circuit into disrepute and these were bought to the attention of the Quarterly Board Meetings, as follows:-

- *"That W...T...having disgraced himself by being connected with smuggling be dismembered."*
- *"That this meeting disapproves of Bro J C's...conduct in getting drunk thereby doing injury to the Cause of God and that he have no appointments this quarter."*
- *"The suspension of Mr C... from Highgate School be continued he having been the worse for drink."*
- *"That Bro C P...be expelled from Society for bad conduct towards his wife turning her out of doors by the hair of her head."*
- *"That this meeting regrets Bro E H...'s indiscretion in following the hounds hunting."*
- *"Bro P... come off the plan for card playing."*
- *"That Bro P... be forgiven his faults."*
- *"That a letter should be sent to Mr S... reproving him for his conduct towards his wife."*
- *"That the name of G C... be removed from the list of local preachers for a serious act of consistency in offering to fight Bro R G... on the high road."*
- *"That friend R... give a written pledge to this quarter and that he beg Bro Y...'s pardon, and promise to mind his own business."*

·*"That the peace pledge shall again be handed to Bros C...and S... and if they sign it, they shall have appointments as usual, and, if not, they shall not have any."*

Neglect of appointments was also considered to be a crime and the following note was in the 1846 plan:- *"that all neglect of appointments, that are not satisfactorily accounted for at the Board, shall be considered wilful neglect, and the delinquent shall have no more appointments on the plan, until he requests them, and promises to take the work faithfully. And if he requests none, his name shall be taken off the plan at the end of six months."*

Occasionally there was a mitigating circumstance, for example, *"that Bro P...'s neglect be overlooked as his feet are lame."*

The demands of the agricultural calendar resulted in the following minutes:- *"that Bro Jackson has liberty to have two Sabbaths in the harvest. That Bro R Pearce have no appointments being a shepherd. That Bro W Sayer have no appointments as he is engaged bullock rearing."*

Recommendations were also made concerning marital affairs, for example, *"That S D... be considered and recommended as a suitable person to become a travelling preacher's wife!"*

And no plumb cake. The Quarterday Meeting dealt with tea meetings and various festivals, which the ladies were expected to prepare, for example:-
(10th September 1847)*"That the preacher's wives provide for the dinner and tea. That tea be provided for 80 and that provisions consist of bread and butter, shrimps, selary and Etc."*
(16th December 1847) *"That there be no quarterday dinner, next quarterday, but there be a publick tea meeting at 6d each and no plumb cake."*
(11th March 1859) *"That there be a quarterday dinner and tea. Cake as usual, 2 legs of mutton, 20 pounds beef, suet 4 lbs."*

(9th September 1859)*"That two legs of mutton small ones and the rest in beef not to exceed 30lbs in whole weight to be had of Bro Coe for quarterday dinner."*
(27th November 1861)*"That there is a quarter dinner Mrs Ballard, and Mrs Clitheroe, Mrs Winfield, Kirk and Coe to help to arrange. Mr Coe provide 36lbs of meat 2 legs of mutton 2 pieces of beef 8 or 9lbs."*
(18th March 1867)*"That two dozen cups and saucers be bought for use at quarterly meeting teas."*
(9th September 1870)*"That Bro Lee speak to Bro Adams about procuring the vegetables for quarterday dinner. That Mrs Rous be affectionately requested to take charge of cooking the quarterday dinner in connection with Mrs Paston, Mrs Sparing, and Mrs Adams. That Mrs K... be informed that as a committee consisting of the preachers wives and Mrs Adams is appointed to provide the quarterday dinner her services will not be required."*

Costs of provisions for the June 1837 meeting were:-

Beer* for Quarter day	4.1
Meat for do dinner	£1.4.6
Bread for Quarter day	5.7 1/2
Tea Bill Quarter day	14.0.

NB.*The cheapest beer available locally was 4d a gallon (source Lynn News 14th September 1844). Thus 4/1d could buy 98 pints of beer.

Conferences at Lynn were held in 1836 and 1844. The 1836 Conference was held behind closed doors and information is unavailable. In 1844 the President was William Clowes and the secretary William Garner. According to Rev. Bell, the camp meeting was *"the People's day."* Thousands attended the services, which were held in a meadow near the 'Hob in the Well'(1). Preparations had begun a year earlier and the accounts show some of the costs including 300 bills @ £2.8.8, 400 plans @ 10/-, 100 tea tickets @ 12/6, 100 plans @ 4/6, 70 dinner tickets @ 2/-. The cost of stationery for the Conference was 7/4 1/2 and the services of a policeman was 2/6d.

The death of a child was a sad case that involved the refusal of an Anglican Minister to inter the corpse of a child that had been baptised by a Primitive Methodist Preacher(2). On 3rd March 1847, Sarah Bowden died. She was the daughter of Thomas Bowden, a Primitive Methodist, and had been baptised by Rev.T.W Rous. At 4pm on 7th March, when the local Priest should have interred the corpse, *"he went in the opposite direction."* The service was eventually conducted by Rev. Richard Howchin on 19th March. He had contacted the Bishop of Norwich and the Committee of Privileges in London, and was advised to bury the child(3).

The First Sunday School started in Lynn on Sunday 2nd October 1825, when 60 children were enrolled. Sunday Schools were run by members of the congregation acting as Sunday School Superintendents. Like all other matters they came under the jurisdiction of the Circuit Committee, for example:-

(17th June 1844) *"That the school have hymn books for rewards at 5d each. That we purchase some cups and saucers for Bro Day and school."*

(13th March 1848) "That the teachers have liberty to give all the Sunday School children a dinner in the middle of June."

A letter written by the Rev.T Lowe, gives details of a Sunday School gala(4).

The Report from Lynn Circuit in March 1849 showed:-

• Lynn	57 teachers	450 children
• Harpley	7 "	35 "
• Rougham	8 "	50 "
• Marham	5 "	30 "
• Fincham	5 "	28 "
• Hollow End	4 "	22 "

Sabbath School Teachers' Plan for 1849 (twenty-four years later) showed that there were 86 teachers and 570 scholars in Lynn, as follows:- New Road (200), Highgate (90), North End (120), Norfolk Street (60) and Infant School (100). A note in the report said *"there is evidence in this plan of organisation and prayer."* The Superintendents were:- Messrs

Plowright, Catton, Bulman, Freeman, and Burrell, J Garner treasurer, H Daisley secretary.

A Connexional Day School was opened at Fincham in 1870 with one teacher and 30 scholars. Receipts for the year were £8.0.9$^1/_2$ - expenditure £5.6.0. It was funded by *"the pence of the children, the profits of a tea meeting, a public collection and subscriptions from different friends."*

Children being children meant that there were occasional problems which were brought to the attention of the Quarterly Meeting, eg *"that an enquiry be made among the Sabbath School teachers as to which of the scholars broke the Chapel gate and if it be ascertained they be made to pay for it."*

A New Sunday School was planned in County Court Road, Lynn, and on 15th September 1875, the foundation stone was laid by Mr William Lift. The inscription from Isaiah said *"And all thy children shall be taught of the Lord."* On 30th April and 1st May 1876, the new school was opened by the Reverend J Ward.

The Reverend J Garner died 17th September 1849 after being a Minister for 22 years. Arrangements made for the funeral included the purchase of twelve crepe and twelve silk hat bands.

The First PM Chapel in London Road was renovated following a trustee's meeting on 8th June 1850 when the following resolutions were agreed:-

1. *"That the front of the gallery be varnished.*
2. *That Mr Suiter whitewash sealing and the walls of the Chapel.*
3. *Mr Panks and Bro..? paint the walls and rooms of the Chapel.*
4. *That the two back pews of the Chapel be converted into free seats.*
5. *That Mrs Sheldrake will clean the Chapel.*
6. *That a note be sent to Mr C... and C... to request them to pay their seat rent or to sit in future on the free seats."*

Further minutes were raised on 18th June 1850, eg.

- *"That the copper be removed out of the house into the yard.*
- *That the old petty be taken from the other side of the Chapel and that Mr Suter do it."*

The building was sold to Mr Green on 8th February 1864, as a fallen mortgage for £80; the full amount of mortgage being £100. The other £20 was transferred to the trustees of the new Chapel.

The New Chapel in London Road was built in 1858 while the Reverend Richard Howchin was Superintendent. St. James Chapel, founded by Bishop Turbus in 1146, originally stood on the site. It became a hospital for poor and impotent people and eventually a Workhouse. One Sunday morning, when most of the inmates were at Church, the building collapsed, killing two people and injuring several others.

After this disaster, Richard Munson Esq, of Walpole purchased the site and sold half the frontage to the Primitive Methodists (108ft x 60ft). A resolution from the minute book dated 30th January 1857, stated *"that Mr Munson be offered five hundred and fifty pounds for the land, and six hundred if he refuse."*

London Road (Photo Brian Hart)

When people became aware of the transaction there were heartburnings in certain quarters when it became known that the finest site in Lynn had been secured for a 'Ranter's' Chapel. Mr Howchin's report said *"that the utmost influence of certain gentlemen of high Church principles was thrown in our way, and had not our undertaking been attended to in business like order, and legally secured, we should have lost our bargain. After the writings were made, and the building nearly ready for the roof, they offered to purchase the whole, if possible, at any price we might fix, so much do some people dislike to see a Primitive Methodist Chapel in so prominent a position."*

The trustees however, held their own, and the present Chapel, designed to accommodate 1000 hearers, was erected on 25th August 1858. Mr Lift was invited to lay a stone, Mr Howchin and Mr Coe to provide a trowel and Mr Howchin to prepare a piece of parchment containing the names of the trustees and Ministers.

The following transcript is a condensed report taken from an 1858 magazine:-

"At 10.30am the Reverend Robert Key preached, and at 12.30 the stone-laying service was begun, the dedication prayer being offered by the Reverend J.T Wigner (Pastor of Stepney Baptist Church). Mr W Lift and others laid stones, many others laid bricks, and the contributions from these that day amounted to nearly £83. At 3 o'clock the Rev. R Key preached again in the old Chapel, and at 5.0'clock, there was a great tea meeting, when over 800 persons sat down, afterwards a meeting was held in Stepney Chapel. The profits on the tea were over £40. On the following day the teachers and scholars in all the then four Primitive Methodist Sunday Schools in Lynn, had a great demonstration. They met on the Tuesday Market Place and formed a circle. They had a saxhorn band, which played the National Anthem, and the Rev. J Broadbent (who was then stationed at Docking) gave an address. After this a procession was formed, headed by the Ministers, the four schools, the band, and a great number of people, finished up with a gaily decorated van that was provided for the smaller children who could not walk the distance. The scene was reported as imposing and the effect powerful and happy. On arriving at the Chapel ground, about 500 children were regaled with the good old English fare of roast beef and plum pudding. (According to Gibbard, £1.16.3 was raised by persons watching the children feed).

The teachers and children afterwards went to the foundation stone and placed £20 on it. The total proceeds from all the services was £145.15.4.

The Chapel opened 31st March 1859, and Rev. R Key preached again. The Rev.Saunderson preached on Sunday 3rd April, and on 10th April, the Rev. W Harland, then Connexional editor, conducted the services. On the Monday he preached an extra service in the afternoon. Approximately 1,100 people came from surrounding villages in the Circuit and sat down to tea (forty trays were given) in the new Chapel, the old Chapel,the Baptist schoolroom, New Connexion schoolroom and the Albion Hall, kindly lent for the occasion. The Wesleyan and Independent Ministers preached on the Sunday afternoons."

The Chapel cost £1,643.15.3$^1/_2$ of which £871 was raised by stone laying, opening services, subscriptions and donations. The Ladies Sewing Society raised £74 and arranged a great bazaar to be opened a few days later.

The Chapel Clock was installed following subscriptions from the public. The Town Council agreed to pay the cost of lighting it at night, which they did for over 40 years. Later, Gibbard wrote, *"the clock is not performing its useful function by night as the Council have cut the gas off."*

As a postscript to this story, the clock was renovated in 1995 and Graham Uttin (Circuit Steward) added electricity and ensured that it was once again lit up at night.

William Lift died on 26th November 1893. The 1894 plan was put in mourning. He had been a member for 65 years, Local Preacher for 61 years and Station Steward for 40 years. William Lift had been one of the earliest scholars when the Sunday School opened in 1825.

A Great Circuit Demonstration was held on August Bank holiday in 1893 at Holme Park. Notice was given of a 'singing contest.'

William Lift

A Great United Camp Meeting was also held in 1893, in Holme Park on 13th August. It was stated that *"the Magdalen Choir will attend. To commence at 8.30."*

Temperance. A Band of Hope was formed at London Road on 5th April 1880, with Messrs Goodson, Savage, Sporne and others as chief officers. The aim was to get young men and women to abstain from drinking alcoholic beverages.

Transport. The following resolutions show how Preachers moved around the Circuit, in addition to walking:-

(4th September 1893) *"That the stewards be authorised to spend a sum of money not exceeding £3 during the next quarter to provide a conveyance on ten Sundays to carry the preachers to Fincham and Massingham and the places near to them, five times each way."*

(7th December 1896) *"That the Rougham and Marham traps be hired from Bro King, but he shall be informed that the preachers refuse to have the chestnut horse. That the traps for the shorter journeys be hired from Huddlestone and Mr Wardle make best arrangements he can."*

(4th July 1904) *"That Societies desiring the services of Lynn preachers Sunday School Anniversary, Chapel Anniversary, or Harvest Festival services are expected to pay for the conveyance and that the amount 6/- be sent to the Circuit Steward in each case."*

(2nd September 1907) *"That Bro W Harkness have not more than two walking journeys, not exceeding four miles each."*

(25th February 1909) *"That we recommend to the Branch quarterly meeting the rearrangement of the traps to the Branch as follows. Instead of three traps to the Branch each quarter from Lynn, conveying 4 preachers each, we arrange for 4 traps as under.*

1 trap from Lynn with 4 preachers for the Branch.

1 trap from Lynn with 2 preachers for the Branch and 2 for St. Mary's and St. German's.

1 trap for Gayton or Grimston with 2 preachers for the Branch and 2 for St. Mary's and St. German's."

(3rd September 1917) "That we make an allowance of 15/- per quarter for railfares to each of the ministers during the two winterquarters."

(1919 plan) *"Traps start from Mr Trenowath's stables."*

(1926 plan) *"Cars to start for the next quarter from opposite Mr Poysers house at 1.15pm."*

Musical Matters. Rules for Village Choirs were established in March 1894. Two of the key rules being as follows:-

1. *"That the choir shall be composed of persons who are either members of our Church*

or of good moral character and of good singing ability.

2. *As singing is an important part of our worship of Almighty God and the choir are the leaders of this Holy exercise, they shall be required to be in their places a few minutes before the time of service, and must observe a reverent attitude and manner in every part of public worship, and all talking or whispering or light or trifling conduct is strictly prohibited."*

A Mission Choir was formed in 1897, supported by members of the Christian Endeavour(5) - for weekends especially. Mr Dines was asked to take the organ on the week nights during the mission. It was proposed that Sankey's Hymns were used and the PSA Committee were asked to

Sunday School Staff c.1905

grant the use of their hymn books. The mission was advertised by posters, circulars and cards.

Some miscellaneous matters of the 20th century

1900. 6th May. District Camp Meeting at Lynn. 7th May. District Meeting tea for which village Societies were asked to provide 20 trays. Lynn friends were asked to provide homes for the delegates and visitors.

Revenue: Total income from all the Chapels in the Circuit, year ending 31st December was £518.0.1 of which £156.12.5 came from pew rents.

1902. Resolution of gratitude and delight at proclamation of peace between Boers and British in South Africa.

1904. Fincham formed as separate Circuit from Lynn on 28th and 29th June. A Circuit Rally held, at the end of which a presentation was made to commemorate the Jubilee of the Reverend G Bell's Ministry, and his retirement from active service.

1905. The Circuit were willing to accept Rev. M.S Cushing as a second preacher for 1905/6 on the understanding that he kept a pony and trap at his own expense to do his journeys. The Rev. Cushing stayed one year.

1907. A Quarterly Meeting held at London Road Church gave the names of those present in the minutes. It consisted of the three Ministers, Revs. W.E Walmsley, F.G Saville and J.H Robertshaw, seven ladies and 22 men; thus a total of 32 people formed the Preachers' meeting. It was then followed by a full Board Meeting and the minutes of the Circuit Committee were received and signed.

1908. Support for the Education and Licensing Bills sent to H.H Asquith, the Prime Minister, and various M.P's.

1911. A P.S.A. Brotherhood meeting was held at London Road Church on the Jan-March Plan. (Pleasant Sunday Afternoon).

1914. The Plan showed 19 Chapels:- London Road, Highgate, North End, Harpley, Rougham, Grimston, Gayton Thorpe, West Newton, Massingham, East Winch, St.German's, Gayton, Terrington, West Winch, Wootton, Clenchwarton, East Walton, St. Mary's, Fair Green.

Each candidate for the plan had to be a total abstainer.

1916. Christmas greetings and a plan were sent to each member serving in His Majesty's Forces. Christmas greetings and a plan were also sent to each conscientious objector,ie P.D...who had been court-martialled and sent to prison for 16 weeks; also F.H... who was in a Dye factory at Huddersfield, under the Pelham Committee.

A Letter of condolence was sent to Mrs Michelborough on the loss she had sustained - her husband having been killed in action on 31st July. (Unfortunately, several such letters were sent).

1919. Letters of welcome were sent on 2nd June, to the men returning from active service.

1921. Resolution and Prayer for 'Peace in Ireland.'

1927. A Great Synod Camp Meeting was held in Lynn on the Walks Recreation Field. The event started at 7.0am on Sunday 1st May, with worship and the sacrament, followed by two processions from the East and South gates, proceeding to the Saturday Market place. There was a Meeting of Witness on the Tuesday Market Place at 1.45pm and a procession to the Camp ground at 2.15pm. Conductors were Revs. Geo E Rudram and A.J Marsh, supported by Messrs G Briggs, G Hindes, F.B Lee and all the preachers on the Circuit Plan. The meeting concluded with community singing in London Road Church at 6.0pm, an Evangelistic Service and a Lovefeast in the school hall at 6.30pm.

Notes:-

(1)Primitive Methodism in King's Lynn Circuit 1821-1904: Rev. G Bell. 1904.

(2)Primitive Methodist Magazine.1847. p.301. The Editor said "It was well-known for some years past, certain men in the Established Church have questioned the validity of what is called 'lay baptism;' but the law upon this question has been decided against them by the superior judge in the ecclesiastical courts, and (on Appeals) by the Judicial Committee of the Privy Council. It is, therefore, now a settled point that baptism, administered with water, and an invocation of the Father, Son, and the Holy Ghost, is valid; and any clergyman refusing to bury the corpse of a parishioner baptised by a dissenting Minister is liable to the punishment of 3 months suspension, and to the payment of costs."

(3)On Tuesday 8th September 1880, the Burials Bill received the Royal Assent and thus passed onto the Statutes. This gave Non-Conformist Ministers the legal right to officiate at funerals in any Churchyard in the Country.

(4)A Letter from Rev.T Lowe to the Editor of the Methodist Magazine:- "On November 5th, 1846, we had a very interesting school gala. In the morning, at ten o'clock, the children in the schools in our town, assembled in the Tuesday Market Place, and from thence, accompanied by their teachers and the travelling preachers, they processioned through some of the principal streets to the Temperance Hall. Each child carried a small flag of various colours; and eighteen large and beautifully textured banners, borne by the teachers, floated gaily on the breeze. After singing and praying in the hall, the children were regaled with a dinner of beef and plum pudding, and seemed not a little pleased with their fair. In the afternoon, about four hundred and twenty four of them, attended by their teachers, were favoured with a trip on the railway (recently opened) to Downham. Eleven carriages formed the train, and crowds assembled to witness the departure and arrival of its juvenile passengers. After a short stay at Downham, they returned safely to Lynn, filling the air with their little hymns as they journeyed; and on their arrival they gave several rounds of hearty cheers on the platform of the terminus.

At five o'clock in the evening, about three hundred persons sat down to an excellent tea, prepared in the hall; and afterwards we had a rich, intellectual and spiritual treat at a public meeting. Mr Lift, one of our local preachers presided; and warm-hearted, powerful, Primitive Methodist addresses were delivered on the importance and advantages of Sabbath School instruction, by the Rev. Mr Hamilton, Independent Minister, Messrs Howchin, Rous, Merry, Burrell, Lincoln and the writer.

We intend to establish a Ragged-Sunday School; a resolution was passed to this effect, at the meeting and excited considerable interest. A school of this kind is greatly needed here; and if it were spiritly taken up, it would soon become one of the greatest blessings to our Circuit.

Great praise is due to the ladies for their activity and good management in providing for the adults and children present at our recent festivity. Recently we have held the anniversary services of the High Street, Highgate and North End schools; and the collecting exceeded those previously realised at these places. Praise God! the converting work has broken out among us and we are expecting a mighty revival." signed. T Lowe

(5)The Christian Endeavour Society began in London Road with Mr W Savage as president. According to Rev. G Bell, there were C.E Societies in Marham, Fincham and Clenchwarton.

Statistics 1837-1932

Year	Members	Trav Preach.	Local Preach.	Chapels & Rooms	Other Places	Sunday Schools
1837	775					
1840	957*					
1845	903*					
1846	782	3	70	3		6
1850	778	2	69	14	15	9
1855	660	2	59	15	13	11
1860	880	4	65	19	11	16
1865	980	4	77	19	13	18
1870	980	4	98	14	22	17
1875	1050	4	97	18	17	20
1879	1090	3	93	21	15	22
1883	1140	3	105	23	13	-
1885	1035	4	96	23	11	-
1890	924	3	90	24	6	21
1895	865	3	99	24	6	-
1900	875	3	120	25	4	-
1905	666	3	85	17	2	-
1910	570	2	67	17	2	-
1915	548	4	70	17	2	-
1920	488	-	-	17	-	-
1926	494	2	73	18	-	-
1930	525	-	-	-	-	-
1932	505	-	-	-	-	-

N.B. In 1932 there were 124 teachers and 786 scholars in the Primitive Methodist Sunday Schools of the Lynn Circuit. A note on the report said "The Sunday Schools are all in a healthy condition, and there are signs of increasing good work in many places."

*These figures include the Docking Circuit.

Chapter four

METHODIST UNION

Some Significant Dates

1933. 5th March was specified as Methodist Exchange and Wesleyans, Primitives and United Methodists exchanged pulpits. The first quarterly meeting of the united Methodist Circuit was held at Tower Street Church on 14th September. The Societies were divided into four sections with the Ministers having pastoral oversight, as follows:-

Rev. C.R Bower:- St. James*, Highgate, Gayton, South Wootton, Harpley, Massingham and West Newton. (*London Road was called St. James to distinguish it from London Road South).

Rev. E Marshall:- Tower Street, North End, Union Lane, West Winch (North and South), Blackborough, Narborough, Pentney and Watlington.

Rev. C.G Oyston:- Terrington Wesley and Popes Lane, Tilney all Saints, Clenchwarton, West Lynn, St. German's, St. Mary's and Saddlebow.

Rev. C.J Clarke:- London Road South, Gaywood, Grimston Wesley, Pott Row, Gayton Thorpe, East Walton, East Winch and Fair Green.

A note on the plan said *"gambling of every kind is expressly forbidden in all Methodist Church buildings by order of Conference. This includes whist drives, guessing and other competitions which involve the principle of the raffle."*

1936. The new Methodist Hymn Book was reported to be in use at all places except Union Lane, West Winch N, Blackborough, Wootton and Saddlebow.

1938. The BI-CENTENARY OF JOHN WESLEY'S CONVERSION was commemorated with Circuit Rallies in Lynn, Terrington and Gayton.

1939. Blackout material was purchased from Messrs Jermyn & Sons.

1940. Lecture at Tower Street 26th February. Subject:- "The Church in wartime."

Only one preacher per Society was supplied on a Sunday, generally at 2.15pm due to the scarcity of petrol and difficulty of travel under "blackout" conditions. It was also considered that if an air raid warning should sound on a Sunday evening it would be far better for folk to be at home than on darkened roads, or gathered in a public building and separated also from those staying at home. St. James, Gaywood, West Newton and Terrington (W) were the only Societies to have two services on the Sunday. All the Societies had an evening service during the week at 6.30. 7 or 7.15pm. During the Summer months, Societies reverted to two services on a Sunday.

1942. A note on the Jan-April Quarterly Guide stated:- *"Watlington - bus leaves library. Train returns from Magdalen Road station 5.5. Tea provided."*

The amount recorded for Overseas Missions (July to Oct Quarterly Guide) was £461.19.2. an increase of £53.1.2.

The wartime restrictions on petrol were making it extremely difficult for preachers to fulfil their engagements. Society Stewards were warned *"even in this present quarter it may become impossible to convey preachers to their destination."*

1943. Tower Street Church was closed for worship, the final services being on 15th August. The view taken was that one central place of worship was adequate for Lynn. Members were asked to transfer to London Road South, Gaywood or other Societies. On 15th August, the order of services was:- 10.45 Morning Service. The Mayor of King's Lynn and the Borough Council attended the service.

6.30pm. Evening Service. Other Lynn Methodist Churches closed for the evening so that the congregations could attend Tower Street.

1945. The Circuit Youth Council replaced the former Circuit Sunday School and Guild Councils and had oversight of all Circuit youth work.

The Lynn Circuit was asked to raise £600 towards the cost of repairing war-damaged Church buildings.

1964. The last service was held at London Road (South) on 30th August.

Statistics 1934-1996

Year	Members	Churches	Rooms: missn
1934	992	30	1:1
1940	958	31	1:1
1945	863	30	1:1
1950	859	29	1:1
1956	745	26	1:0
1961	706	24	-
1965	722	22	-
1971	602	17	-
1975	598	16	-
1980	581	15	-
1985	544	15	-
1990	558	15	-
1996	439	13	-

Chapter five

CLENCHWARTON

The Wesleyan Methodists. On 17th and 18th June 1833, a piece of land 45 feet by 38 feet, common land before enclosure, was sold for £6 by John Crane to nine trustees for a Wesleyan Methodist Chapel to be built on the site(1). It was bounded by land belonging to William Palmer Morowood, the public road towards the South, and the land belonging to Sarah Wardle.

The earliest available record of a Society appeared in September 1838; Clenchwarton being credited with 17 members. In 1843, Sister Scarfe was the Society Steward.

The Primitive Methodists first available record of a Society appeared in 1838 when five un-named people were registered as "on trial." It is recorded that they paid 3/0½ quarterage. By 1844, this Society had grown to 26 people who during the year contributed a total of £3.9.9 to the Circuit(2).

During 1844, Camp Meetings and Revival Meetings were planned in several places, including Clenchwarton. On 4th February 1844, Abigail Alexander, daughter of Robert and Susan, was baptised by the Rev. John Winkfield.

Rev. John Winkfield

In December 1844, it was recorded *"that Mr Winkfield and Hawes have liberty to enquire about a piece of land at Clenchwarton for Chapel."* Nothing materialised, so in September 1845, it was agreed *"that Clenchwarton Chapel concern be taken up by Mr Howchin."*

Camp Meetings were again held during 1846 and 1847. During the latter year it was planned *"that a tea meeting be held at Clenchwarton, Mr Howchin's next appointment."*

During 1848, Clenchwarton came "off the plan" (reason unknown) and the travelling preacher was asked *"to attend to Clenchwarton preaching house."* In March 1849, it was agreed *"that Clenchwarton come on the plan and two preachers planned."* Minutes of 11th March 1850, recorded *"that Clenchwarton preaching be at Mr Cuninghams house and the class led by the preachers*(3)*."*

Minutes in June 1850 recorded *"that the Society at Clenchwarton keep at Bro Cunninghams house."* and *"that the preachers lead the class and that Bro Hawes be requested to meet in the class."*

On 15th September 1851, the Circuit Committee at last had some good news when it was agreed *"that this meeting gratefully accept the offer of Mr Briggs to give a piece of land for a Chapel at Clenchwarton and that the Travelling Preachers attend to it immediately."*

Meanwhile, the trustees of the Wesleyan Chapel, having found the financial burden too onerous, (one member had died and two had emigrated to America), had asked the Wesleyan Conference for permission to sell their property. This was granted on 18th July 1854, by the Conference Chairman, John Lomas. On 11th August 1856, the Chapel and land were sold by Robert Tubbs, etc, to Rev. Wainwright, a Primitive Methodist Travelling Preacher.

Rev. W Wainwright

The First P.M. Chapel (purchased from the Wesleyan Methodists) cost £34.11.6d. The total debt when the Chapel was completed was £27.0.0. It could accommodate

130 people - 86 in pews and 44 in free seats. The average attendance at the principal Sunday services was 60, and there was an average of 30 hearers on weekdays. The estimated value was £60 and Mr Lincoln was the treasurer of this freehold property. Mrs Barwood collected the seat rents. There were no members in the Society when the Chapel was purchased. (There is also a gap in the Circuit accounts book from 13th September 1852 to 15th December 1856, when, on this date, no members are shown but 2/0½d was collected).

Brother Rowland was given permission to speak in June 1861, and the preacher was asked to see the Society and *"if they are agreeable he become the leader of the class."*

In 1862, the trustees were asked to reduce their debt, if practicable. They were also allowed to erect *"a privy"* at the back of the Chapel.

On 14th September 1863, Miss Rogers was requested to assist at the Chapel Anniversary.

In 1865 the Authorities agreed *"that a new stove be bought for Clenchwarton."*

An example of how closely the Circuit Committee were controlling the Societies affairs was illustrated in January 1867, as follows:- *"the Clenchwarton Chapel cleaner be paid 1/- more a quarter than heretofore - and they have a week's protracted meetings."* Later, in October, *"that a person at Clenchwarton be offered £1 a year to clean and light the Chapel, etc,that Mr Lincoln see to the matter."*

In 1867, Brother Rowland, the Class Leader, was mildly admonished for announcing a Temperance Meeting to be held in the Chapel without obtaining the sanction of the Circuit Committee. A few months later, the Rev. Howchin was to write a letter of commendation and credentials for him and his wife, following their move from the village.

On 23rd October 1867, Mr Cox was appointed Leader and Mr Warnes,

Assistant Leader, of the Society.

The Circuit Committee decided to insure the Chapel for £100 in 1869, with the Primitive Methodist Insurance Company. A decision was also taken at the same meeting for Brother Suiter to clean and repair the Chapel.

In November 1869, a demand was received from Clenchwarton Parish Council who had assessed the Chapel for Poor rate and Mr Lift was asked to obtain the advice of the General Committee. A week later, Mr Worth was dispatched to Wisbech to get the Chapel registered and the following action was resolved:- *"that a Poor Rate having been assessed on Clenchwarton Chapel we deem it inexpedient to pay it as such a place is exempt by law. If Br Lincoln be summoned on account thereof he be at liberty to defend an action at law, and may employ lawyer Dawbarn of March."*

A Chapel Anniversary was held on 22nd September 1872. There was good financial news in 1878,as follows:- *"that the Clenchwarton Chapel having become debtless, the Trustees and Circuit Committee cojointly manage their concerns."* A year later Mr Lincoln was asked to invest the balance of £30 held by him as treasurer.

The second Chapel (Photo Brian Hart)

On 9th June 1879, a committee consisting of Messrs Seaman, Lift, Ballard and Lincoln, considered the *"refraining or rebuilding"* of the Chapel with a result that on 6th September 1880, the Society were given permission to build a new Chapel. Six months later on 14th March 1881, the Authorities applied to the District Building Committee for sanction to build; specifications to be approved by the Station Committee. On the same day a new trust was formed(4). A week later the Authorities approved of the specifications and plans, having indicated some design modifications to the architect, Mr Hillam. They also decided the fate of the old Chapel in that *"failing to get the old Chapel taken down by the people themselves the offer of Mr Riches to pull it down for 50/- be accepted."*

The New Chapel stone-laying ceremony was performed on 5th October 1881, by Mr William Lift, Circuit Steward. The Chapel was opened by Rev.J Smith on 22nd January 1882. The cost was £261. There were 120 sittings and 50 adherents. On Monday 23rd January, Rev. Graham gave a sermon at 3pm; a public tea and meeting followed.

In June 1894, Brother Kidd was asked to furnish the next Quarterly Meeting with his documents with a view to his name appearing on the plan as a preacher on trial.

New trustees were appointed on 12th September 1895(5). In this year, permission was given for the Mission Band to go to Clenchwarton. A year later, the institution of the Christian Endeavour was sanctioned.

Temperance. A Band of Hope Anniversary was held in 1896. There was a juvenile Band of Hope in 1900 with 50 total abstainers.

Total Income in 1900, was £17.13.11d which included £2.7.0 pew rents and £1.0.0 school rent.

Sister Butter and Brothers J Butter and W.S Lane came on the plan as note holders in 1902. Mr W.S Lane was received on to the full plan as a Lay Preacher on 9th March 1914. In 1921, a note of liberty was given to his son Mr W.S.F Lane with a request that *"he accompany his father."* In 1933 he came a fully accredited Local Preacher.

The third generation of the Lane family, Mr Alan Lane, became a Local Preacher in 1966. His sister, Mrs Barbara Smith, has been an organist at the Chapel for over 50 years and her husband, Mr Harold Smith, has been a Local Preacher since 1954.

Clenchwarton had a week's mission in October 1937, conducted by Messrs Shinfield, Leggett, Medlock, J.H Watts and A Thurston. A fête took place on 23rd July 1938, at Manor Farm in aid of the building fund.

The Sunday School 1863-1900. In 1863 there were 11 teachers and 70 scholars; in 1865, 9 teachers and 51 scholars and in 1871, 8 teachers and 48 scholars. In 1875, Mr Lewis was superintendent and Mr Cox treasurer. Mr W.S Lane was secretary in 1897 and Mr W Warren in 1899. In 1900, there were 9 teachers and 44 scholars and Clenchwarton was the venue for the Circuit Sunday School Conference.

In 1918, the Circuit Committee sent a deputation consisting of the Rev.A Banham, and Brothers W.J Burnell, J Denny, J Reeve, V.A Crawford and A Crawford, to visit and *"enquire what can be done to resuscitate the Sunday School."*

The Circuit Sunday School Conference was held on Saturday 23rd October 1920. President of the afternoon sessions was Mrs E Hipkins, and papers were given by Miss K Pratt and Mr E.J Fuller. There was a public tea at 5pm and a platform meeting at 7pm, in which Mr W.J Burnell was the Chairman. The speakers included:- E Isbell, S Rasberry and W Bland. Proceeds were for the Circuit deficit.

On 31st October 1957, there were 7 teachers and 92 scholars in the Sunday School, which met in the Chapel on the Sunday morning. (There was an afternoon service at 2.30 and an evening service at 6.30).

In 1959, a gift of land by Mr Jack Ogden of Porch Farm, Clenchwarton, (keeping his late father's promise), enabled a Sunday School room (108'x60') to be built adjoining the Chapel. The stone was laid by Mr A.V Hilton M.P.(later Lord Hilton) on 14th October 1961. He said that *"it was a definite act of faith in these days to build a Sunday School."*

From plans by Warren Bros. it was built by R.H Clare Ltd at a total cost of £2,577. The opportunity was taken to restructure the Chapel by installing a new entrance, bricking up the original and moving the altar. It was opened on 20th January 1962 by Mrs James Cooper, wife of a Minister of the Methodist Church. Chairman was Alderman Hunter Rowe Esq, J.P.

On 28th September 1976, a lorry crashed into the schoolroom causing extensive damage. After repairs, the schoolroom re-opened on 5th December, the same year.

The Chapel Centenary occurred in 1981. A monthly programme of events started on 11th October lasting a year.

Refurbishment and gifts. In the Chapel are:- 56 new chairs, purchased in 1979, replacing the old pews; a tapestry of the Last Supper, made by Mr Peter Allen; pictures of Israel, presented by Mrs June Warren; a memorial inscription by Mr Vic Fuller, (the wood used was formerly in the New Connexion Chapel in Ferry Road); a Cross, made by Mr Tom Warren; a lectern, made by Mr W.S.F Lane; the altar cloth, made by Mrs K Clarke; brass and commemorative plates, presented by Mr Lambert; a brass swan flower container, donated by C.M.E.G in memory of Mrs Edith Shaw. The Communion rail was previously in St.Albans Boundary Road Methodist Church. Refurbishment has included, in the Chapel:- overhead electric heaters, a new floor, carpeting and electronic organ, and in the schoolroom:- double glazing, night storage heaters and foam insulation in the ceiling.

Christmas day c.1972(L Lane)

Society Stewards 1882-1996 include:- W Cox, J Kidd, W.S Lane, T Cox, J Butter, T Daines, O Bowden, A Naylor, Arthur Naylor, J English, J Warren, K Meek, R Bocking, A Lane, J.G Jones, A Gadsden, W.S.F Lane, B Gadsden, H.D Smith.

Organisations include:- the Youth Club, Mens' Fellowship (started 1979), Entertainment Group (CMEG - started 1984), Womens' Friendly hour (started 1979), Study Group and Home Communion, Alpha course.

Membership in the mid - Victorian era, fluctuated from a high of 26 to a low of five (1848). During the 20th century membership has been as follows:-

1901 - 20	1927 - 11	1954 - 22	1981 - 19
1905 - 19	1934 - 09	1961 - 20	1986 - 28
1912 - 18	1939 - 14	1965 - 23	1990 - 28
1917 - 10	1944 - 15	1971 - 26	1996 - 23
1922 - 08	1949 - 20	1976 - 29	

A new trust was formed on 28th November 1960. The Chairman was Rev. Ernest Partner.

The Community Roll in June 1996, included 21 members, plus 21 non-members who worship regularly. There were 30 children in the Sunday School and Youth Group.

Prayer Meeting 1992 (Photo H Smith)

Notes:-
(1)These were Mathew Johnson, George Cooper, James Cozens, William Bowler, John Learmouth, Thomas Cullen, Robert Tubbs, William Gilbert and William Gray.
(2) The 1844 Society comprised:- Jonathan Haws Leader, Sarah Haws, Robert Alexander, Susan Alexander, James Tann, Harriet Tann, Sarah Welton, James Haythorpe, Abigail Haythorpe, Robert Tann, William Clitheroe, Alice Cox, Sarah Cox, Charlotte Cunningham, Frederick Harrison, Susan Youngs, May Ann Ray, William Gibson, John Hewett, Elizabeth Youngs, Matthew Claxton, Ann Clithero, Robert Bruse, William Sutterby, Susan Hay.
(3)The 1851 census showed two Robert Cunninghams living in Clenchwarton:-

Robert Cunningham of 8, Cotton Row, 40, shoemaker, born Hardingham, wife Charlotte, born Wreningham, (a member). Robert Cunningham, 42, ag. labourer, born St. Peter, Suffolk, wife Amelia.

(4)The 1881 trust consisted of:- James Kidd gardener and Thomas Bowden farmer, both of Clenchwarton, Thomas Lincoln broker, Nathaniel Ballard butcher, John Goodson labourer, William Mays butcher, Frederick J Head butcher, George Winkfield shoemaker and George Hammond coal dealer, all of Lynn.

(5)The 1898 trust consisted of the following continuing trustees:- James Kidd gardener of Lynn, Thomas Bowden farmer of Clenchwarton, John Goodson labourer, and George Hammond gentleman, both of Lynn and the following new trustees:- Richard B Studd poulterer, Thomas Huddlestone shoemaker, James Henry Martin fruiterer, Richard Samuel Tipple tailor, all of Lynn, and Thomas Davies coachman and Henry John Butter farmer, both of Clenchwarton.

Chapter six

GAYTON

The Wesleyan Methodists' earliest available record show a Society in 1837 with 21 members. By 1843 this had risen to 68. In 1838, class leaders were listed as Barker and Harrison. In 1840 the Society Steward was given as S/r Harrison. There is mention of a Chapel in existence in 1870.

By 1895 the membership had fallen to 21. A high point of 29 members was reached in 1902. The Society merged with the ex Primitive Methodists in 1933.

The Primitive Methodists earliest available record indicate that preaching took place in a Chapel in the Back Street, hired from Mr Goward.

In March 1845, a Missionary meeting was planned by the Circuit Authorities and later in the September, it was agreed that *"Gayton have an anniversary on the plan by Mr and Mrs Howchin."* In the Summers of 1846 and 1847, Camp Meetings were planned and during 1848, a Revival Meeting was held.

Brothers E Symonds and J Rasberry came on the plan as Prayer Leaders and Exhorters in 1863. Brothers J Walden and F Daw also came on the plan as Prayer Leaders. On 12th December 1864, it was agreed *"that a note of liberty be given to Miss L Daw of Gayton.* Mark Hanslip was given a note of liberty in September 1865.

March 1867, heralded the sign of an intention to build a Chapel, as follows:- *"that we entertain the matter of a new Chapel for Gayton - authorise the purchase of land for the same - apply to the District Building Committee for sanction to take steps towards the erection of a new Chapel and kindly request Mr Meek of Gayton, when in Lynn Tuesday, 16th to wait upon Mr Lincoln, Mr Rous also being present, that we may understand full particulars respecting his offer to sell us a piece of land."*

A cautionary statement was issued by the Circuit Committee on 26th June 1867, ie *"that the Committee think it premature on behalf of the Gayton Friends to attempt to purchase land at present."*

During 1868, there was no agreement to purchase a piece of land, despite a further interview between William Lift, the Circuit Steward, and Mr James Meek.

In February 1869, in an interview with a Mr H.... of Gayton, the Circuit Committee authorised the negotiators *"to offer the enormous sum of £60 for a piece of land 60 feet wide by 40 feet long."* This meeting was also unfruitful as the following minute suggests:- *"that a note be sent to Mr H... informing him that the Committee respectfully decline his offer respecting the purchase of his land."*

Rev. J.T.W Rous

Then, on 15th December 1869, Brothers Rous and Lincoln were requested to go to Gayton, *"to purchase ground for a new chapel if they can secure a suitable piece for £45 on condition £5 be returned as a donation."* Also it was agreed that the plans and specifications for Shouldham should be examined with a view to seeing if *"they will do"* for the intended Chapel.

During the next quarter, the Circuit Committee actively raised money by collecting cards, while the minister, the Rev. Howchin, discussed plans and specifications with Mr Hillam, the architect. The committee decided *"that the rent be payed for the rented Chapel in the Back Street, and notice given to leave it."*

On 27th April 1870, it was agreed *"that Mr Howchin arrange for holding District Meeting at Gayton for the purpose of laying before them the plans and specifications for new Chapel."* An advertisement for tenders was placed in both Lynn Newspapers and Mr Howchin was asked to write to suitable Builders bringing the advertisement to their attention; tenders to be in by 25th May.

On 4th June 1870, there was the conveyance of a piece of land from Mr James Meek to Mr David Burton and others for a Primitive Methodist Chapel for the sum of £50(1). It was bounded by the turnpike road and land owned by Edward Everard and James Meek.

Just over a week later, the Committee asked the Reverends Howchin and Rous (the Ministers), *"to go to Gayton to set out the land."* Brother James Symonds was asked to preach at the foundation stone laying on 6th July and the Committee agreed to purchase a book on which *"to record all particulars respecting Gayton new Chapel."*

Gayton Chapel (photo Brian Hart)

The contract for building the new Chapel was awarded to Mr Bardell of Middleton for the sum of £223. On 22nd June 1870, the meeting decided *"that the Gayton Chapel contract must not be broken under any circumstances whatever and the work shall proceed forthwith as first fixed upon by the builders and R Howchin, J.T.W. Rous"* (the Superintendent Minister).

James Symonds was confirmed as the preacher at the stonelaying ceremony on 22nd June 1870. It was planned to follow this with a tea meeting at the Wesleyan Chapel in Gayton, with tickets 9d each. William Lift was asked to lay the foundation stone.

During the Summer the Society was written to, asking, *"if anyone of them intends to provide the Chapel with a cushion and Bible for the rostrum as if not, one is promised."*

In September it was agreed that begging cards be printed for Gayton and to apply for Mr Shields to preach sermons at the opening of the Chapel on Sunday and following Monday, 16th and 17th October, in conjunction with the Rev. Howchin. Later that month Mr Rous was asked to order six lamps for the new Chapel.

Monies advanced on mortgage at 5 per cent included the following:- £150 from a Lodge interest paid to J Nurse solicitor, £30 from the Rev F. B. Paston and £20 from James Hillen.

The Chapel cost £350. The Ministers let the seats and the Superintendent was treasurer. There were 240 sittings and 180 adherents.

Mr Lift was asked to advance £100 to Mr Bardell of Middleton, and the Committee agreed *"that he be repayed this day week, or sooner if the money be forthcoming."* In December, Gayton Sabbath School were asked to pay rent of £2 to the new Chapel.

In 1871, Gayton Friends were offered the iron fence belonging to North End property, at a fair valuation, for erection in front of their new Chapel. At the December Circuit Meeting, the same year, it was agreed *"that a public collection be appointed at Gayton one Sunday next quarter for coco nut matting"* and, *"that Mr Gunns pays Mr Lift the sum he has expended for the pallisading for the Chapel."*

In September 1872, Mr Gunns was asked to look into the rebuilding of the dilapidated wall adjoining the Chapel.

Brother Reeder was given liberty to speak on 10th September 1875.

The Society were sanctioned to hold a Temperance meeting on 1st January 1879.

In June 1880, the Trustees obtained approval to have their Chapel cleaned and Mr Metcalf's tender was accepted for the work.

The Circuit Committee approved the purchase of additional land on 30th March 1881 and at the Quarterly meeting it was agreed *"that we sanction the purchase of land at Gayton for a schoolroom and that the Trustees prepare their arrangements to build and present them to next Quarterly meeting."*

The June Circuit Committee resolved *"that the matter of purchasing a piece of land for the extension of Gayton Chapel, be left with Messrs Smith and Lift."* The Trustees were also given permission *"to build a boundary wall along side of their Chapel and liberty to use such means as they deem best to raise the money, but the matter shall stand in abeyance till Mr Wardle can meet the Trustees and will then arrange for the work to be done, that Mr Tempest get begging cards printed for the same."*

On 27th September 1882, there was an agreement between Mr James Meek senior and John Smith of King's Lynn, acting for the Chapel Trustees, involving the sale of a piece of land adjoining the Primitive Methodist Chapel, 81 feet x 3 feet on the South side of the Chapel and 33 feet x 15 feet at the back of the chapel, at the rate of 5/- per yard, with a deposit of £5 in part payment.

In 1896, new Trustees were appointed(2).

Events in 1899 included a request that the Sunday School teachers contribute to the Sunday School Union, a proposed visit from Mr Wardle to organise a Christian Endeavour Society, and a Band of Hope Anniversary. The Society were also given sanction to renovate their Chapel. A Marriage Certificate was issued on 22nd September, and

Worship Registration Certificate on 9th September. (An earlier Worship Certificate had been issued on 13th April 1874).

Total Income in 1900 was £20.17.3. This included £8.10.0 seat rents, £1.5.0 School rent, and £1.5.0 Anniversary collection.

On 30th November 1904, Mr W Howard came on the full plan, having passed a satisfactory examination.

In Memory of the late Mr John Rasberry the trustees were allowed to place a tablet in the Chapel, in March, 1908. Later sanction was given for the names of Messrs James and Charles Rasberry to be added to the tablet. Permission was given in 1909, for another tablet to the memory of Mr Oliver Rasberry.

During 1908 Mr Stanley Rasberry and Mr Sydney Daws were granted notes of liberty and the Trustees were given permission to build a boundary wall at the end of the Chapel and to hold a bazaar for the same on Easter Monday, 1909.

A Circuit Camp Meeting at Gayton was planned for 7th July, 1909 and twenty-seven brethren were asked to take part. The programme included:-

10am.	Procession to the Camp ground.
10.30am.	Service.
12 o'clock.	Luncheon.
1.15pm.	Procession.
2 o'clock.	Camp meeting.
4 o'clock.	Tea.
5.15pm.	Open air meeting and procession.
6pm.	Lovefeast in Chapel, and Evangelistic Service in Jubilee Hall.

The price for lunch was not to exceed 1/- and the tea was to be 6d. The provision of lunch and tea was left with the Society at Gayton.

Mr R.W Pamment was invited with the London Road and Circuit Choirs. Programmes with suitable hymns were prepared, to be sold at 1d each, and services were advertised in the Circuit magazine.

An invitation was extended to Societies of neighbouring Circuits and arrangements were made for conveyances to leave Lynn at 9am and 1pm.

Following the successful outcome, the Committee planned a Centenary Camp meeting at Gayton for 29th May 1910.

A Circuit Rally was planned at Gayton on Monday 20th June, in aid of the Circuit deficit. The Rev. J.H Robertshaw was asked to preach at 3.30 in the afternoon, with a public tea at 5.30 and meeting in the evening. The Societies in number 2 section were asked to provide trays for the tea as part of their contribution to the deficiency fund. The rally was to be arranged by the junior steward and Mr Twite.

On 4th December 1911, it was resolved that Brothers S Rasberry and H Scase were to be publicly received as Local Preachers. In 1912, Brothers Garrett and Shinn were elected leaders of a newly formed class.

Gayton PM Sunday School c.1905

In 1913, Brother Crow was received on the full Plan. However, the Society pre-empted events because at the June meeting it was resolved *"that a letter be sent to the Gayton Society strongly condemning the action of the Friends who arranged for the recognition service of Bro Crow, thus violating rule 444 of the General Rules 1912. By their action they have prevented Bro Crow from having a public official recognition."*

Approval was given in 1917, for both classes of the Society to meet together on Wednesday nights.

In June 1918, the Society asked for a second Camp Meeting to be held and the proceeds given to the Red Cross; this was not approved.

Gayton Local Preachers in 1926 were:- F Daws, W.G Shinn, W Patrick, H Scase, S Rasberry, L Crow and G Shinn.

On 31st March 1933, 18 Trustees were appointed for the Chapel. There was the conveyance of a piece of land at the rear of the Chapel to the Trustees from H.R Dann, for the sum of £30 on 5th April 1934. On 7th and 22nd September 1960, 18 trustees were appointed for land and Chapel.

Sunday School. On 15th March 1847, the Circuit Authorities decided there should be a Sabbath School at Gayton. This became a flourishing concern and in 1865 there were 15 teachers and 81 scholars. In 1871, 21 teachers, but the number of scholars had declined to 75. In 1897, Mr James Rasberry was Sunday School secretary.

There were 25 teachers and 93 scholars in 1900, with an average attendance of 76. (Twenty-five of the scholars were reported as being over the age of 14 years.)

P.M Membership in the Mid 19th Century, recorded between 1842 and 1848 averaged around 35, with a high point of 68 in the second quarter of 1844.

Membership 1900-1996

1900. 50.	1933. 46.	1960. 26.	1990. 13.
1905. 61.	1935. 42.	1965. 26.	1994. 10.
1912. 58.	1940. 40.	1970. 15.	1996. 09.
1917. 43.	1945. 29.	1975. 15.	
1920. 41.	1950. 30.	1980. 13.	
1925. 33.	1955. 35.	1985. 12.	

PM Society Stewards from 1879:- James Rasberry senior, James Rasberry junior, T Bunkall, J Gidney, J Howard, W Patrick, W Bland, W Reed, E Howard, Mrs Howard, Miss J Rasberry, G Neal, D Shinn, Mrs P Suckling, K Neal.

In 1933 it was announced that *"the two Methodist Societies at Gayton have united and services are held in the Ex-Prim Chapel."* The Ex Wesleyan Chapel was sold in 1935.

Special Events included a Camp meeting planned for 25th July 1937, with Messrs F Medlock, S Marshall and G Shinn.

A Special Event Circuit Rally was held in 1938, the Bi- Centenary of John Wesley's Conversion. (Circuit Rallies were also held at Lynn and Terrington).

A fête, opened by the Countess of Romney, took place on 9th July 1938 in Gayton Hall Park. Another fête, for Trust funds, occurred on Saturday 12th July 1947.

Notes:-

(1) The 11 Trustees who signed the Indenture in 1870, were:- David Burton wheelwright, Mark Hanslip, James Rasberry, Charles Rasberry, John Rasberry, Thomas Walden, Elizah Symonds, Francis Daws, James Howard, William Howard, Thomas Bunkle.

(2) The new and continuing Trustees consisted of :- Robert Wilson engineman, James Rasberry carrier, Charles Rasberry, Frances Daw, Arthur Howard labourer, James Howard labourer, John Howard labourer, Clement Howard labourer, Benjamin Daws labourer, George Shinn bailiff, George Petch labourer, Henry Bunkall shoemaker, Thomas Bunkall.

Chapter seven

GAYWOOD

The Wesleyan Methodist records show a Society in 1839 with 10 members. A Chapel was built in 1874 (now the Evangelical Church) and a Trust formed on 8th April 1874(1). Trusts were also formed in 1919(2) and 1920(3).

Wesleyan Membership

1885 - 32 1890 - 17 1895 - 28 1900 - 23 1905 - 36	1910 - 27 1915 - 36 1920 - 34 1925 - 41 1930 - 33

The Primitive Methodists had a membership of 10 in 1840, 8 in 1843, varied from 26 to 15 in 1844, and fell from 11 to zero in 1845.

The Circuit Authorities decided *" that Gaywood come off the Plan"* on the 15th September 1845. A Revival Meeting was planned for November 10th 1846.

On 16th March 1863, it was resolved *"that Gaywood come on the Plan for a Sunday evening appointment."* Just over one month later and it was agreed, *"that the Committee do not see its way clear to form a class at Gaywood at present, but will consider the matter and make enquiries."*

A Meeting held in September 1864 decided *"that an enquiry be made at Gaywood prior to the Plan coming out relative to the house being closed (and if against us) the place come off the Plan."*

Membership after Union

1935 - 38 1940 - 44 1945 - 45	1950 - 78 1955 - 72 1960 - 91	1965 - 145 1970 - 117 1975 - 145	1980 - 166 1985 - 169 1990 - 168 1996 - 123

Society Stewards 1933 -1990

A Green, J Lusher, J Hewitt, G Blanchflower, F Free,
A Boyce, L.W.A Barrett, T.C Tuck, Miss E Uren,
C.J Young, Miss E Akers, Miss B Mallett, G Coldham,
Miss J Drake, T.J Fry, D Teale, I.P Evans,
V Price Jones, P Mason, G Eeles, Mrs W Kenyon,
R Stephenson, D Baldry, R.J Cooke, M Bashton,
Mrs D Horrex, A Chilvers, J Moorhouse, G Greening,
G Wrenn, J Stent, Mrs L Warrener.

Significant events included a Circuit garden party held at "Vallette", Gaywood, in 1940, by kind permission of Mr and Mrs J.M Barrett, for the reduction of the Circuit debt.

New Trusts were formed on 30th January 1948 and 20th January 1964.

Gaywood Anglican/Methodist Sharing Scheme. Following the closure and sale of Tower Street Methodist Church in 1943, the money was earmarked for a new Methodist Church at Gaywood. A building fund-raising committee was formed and a site purchased in Field Lane. A number of schemes were prepared but none of them reached fruition. Meanwhile, the establishment of periodic services with the Anglicans in the 1960's led to the appointment of a small group to discuss the joint needs of the community. One successful project started was the "Forget-Me-Not-Club" which went from strength to strength with Mrs Boxall and then Mrs Kenyon with their band of loyal helpers.

At a critical time, when the Methodists were desperate for larger premises, the Anglicans offered glebe land behind the Churchrooms on which a new Methodist Church and Rooms could be built. However, before any building work could go ahead the 1969 Churches Sharing Agreement was passed which led to the Rector and the P.C.C. inviting the Methodists to enter a sharing agreement with them for the joint use of the Parish Church.

In February, 1974, the Methodists closed their Church and crossed the road to worship in the Parish Church. Later, under a joint building agreement, the Gaywood Church Rooms were erected.

Notes:-

(1) Members of the 1874 Trust were:- William Thompson the elder, William L Armes manufacturer's agent, Alfred Jermyn draper, Jonathan Richardson Cossons hatter, Robert Whiteman baker,Jonathan Ashton Hillam stonemason, Robert Bush baker, Thomas Ashby Jackson manufacturer's agent, Robert Crane landowner, Daniel Barnard fish agent, James Kirkby Riggall farmer.

(2)Members of the Trust c.1919 were:- Alfred Jermyn, Jonathan R Cossons, Robert Bush, W.R Smith, Frederick A Curson, James Smith, S.A Smyth, R.S Smith, W.T Hayes, C.G Barrett, J.M Barrett, Hubert A Jermyn, B.W Jermyn.

(3)Members of the Trust listed c.1920:- Alfred Jermyn, Samuel Best, William Robert Smith, Robert Stephen Smith, William Thomas Hayes, Charles Golding Barrett, James Morgan Barrett, Bertrand William Jermyn, Hubert Alfred Jermyn, Arnold Green, Bernard Victor Smith, Henry James Purser, John Edward Bossingham, Robert Johnson, John Pilling, Alfred Claxton Dye, Hugh Robert Croot, John Henry Dew, Henry Sheldon, Edward George Flowerday.

Chapter eight

GRIMSTON and POTT ROW

(The Wesleyan Chapel at Grimston and the Primitive Chapel at Pott Row were both known as Grimston, or sometimes "Grimstone").

The Wesleyan Methodist records show that a Chapel was leased for one year on the 9th October 1811, followed by *"appointment and release land"* on the following day. On 25th March 1812, the word *"mortgage"* appears in the records, followed three days later by *"bargain and sale."*

On 21st March 1836, the Chapel was leased for one year (this may or may not refer to the original Chapel).

Chapel trustees, listed in the Circuit Schedule Book for 1837-1843 were:- Wm Clare, Henry Gamble, Wm Lyre, Wm Gilbert, J Clare, Thos Broadbent and Wm Spooner. In 1837, the 23 members were divided into three classes and the leaders were:- Mr Chesson (9), Wm Jessop (7), and Henry Gamble (7). Between 1837 and 1843 the membership fluctuated between 16 and 25.

In 1838 the Society Steward was Mr Clare; Mrs Clare filled the post in 1840. "Grimstone" was listed as having a Chapel with 200 sittings.

New trustees were appointed in 1876(1).

Grimston Wesleyan membership 1885- 1955

1885 - 33	1910 - 12	1936 - 16
1890 - 26	1915 - 16	1940 - 12
1895 - 30	1920 - 15	1945 - 14
1900 - 22	1925 - 10	1950 - 09
1905 - 12	1930 - 08	1955 - 10

The former Wesleyan Chapel was sold in 1981 for £5,485.12. Total income for the year 1980-81 was £196.22 which was used mainly for various charities. The account was closed on 31st August 1981.

The Primitive Methodist recorded 12 members in 1838 with John

Collinson as Class Leader(2). Between December 1836 and 1848, membership fluctuated between a low of 9, in 1838 and 1839 and a high of 75 in the second quarter of 1844.

On 19th March 1845, a missionary meeting was planned at Grimston and Camp Meetings were planned in 1848 and 1849. The Travelling Preachers and Brethren were asked to *"investigate Grimston land for Chapel affair"* in 1851.

Pott Row Chapel(Photo Brian Hart)

The First Chapel cost £78.14.6¾ when built in 1857. There were 20 members. The freehold Chapel could seat 80 in pews and 40 in free seats. The principal services on Sunday were attended by 110 people and the average number of hearers on weekdays was 40. A Sabbath School used the premises rent free. Annual income in 1859 was £6.5.8¼ of which £5.4.6. was raised from pew rents.

On 13th December 1862, a letter was sent to the Class Leader *"affectionately requesting him to be more active in collecting his weekly pence of his members, and strongly recommending all to pay, that are able."*

The Chapel may have been overcrowded at peak services and in June 1863, the Circuit Meeting resolved *"that Mr Scott enquire into the propriety of enlarging Grimstone Chapel."*

Then, on 23rd August 1871, it was resolved *"that the request for a new*

Chapel at Grimstone be entertained and the case be recommended to the consideration of the quarterly meeting." A joint effort ensued between the Travelling Preachers and the Grimston Society to obtain a piece of land. On 7th April 1875, it was agreed *"that Mr Seaman and Mr Lift be authorised to negotiate for the purchase of property for a Chapel at Grimstone."* Success led to agreement on 14th June 1875, *"that the meeting approves the purchase of land and cottages at Grimstone by Messrs Seaman and Lift and sanctions application to the District Building Committee."* One month later, it was decided *"that a trust be formed for Grimstone property, and collecting cards be issued forthwith."*

Trust members were appointed on 11th August 1875(3). On the same date Mr Seaman, the Superintendent Minister, was asked to *"try to borrow what money may be necessary to complete the above purchase".*

The meeting on 10th September resolved *"that a Harvest Home tea meeting be held at Grimstone on Thursday week - to call in the new Chapel collecting cards - and Mr Seaman attends with Mr Rudram."* The same meeting minuted, *"that we advise the trustees of the new Chapel at Grimstone in connection with the Circuit Committee - to take steps to build as soon as they see the way clear - and that instructions be given for getting out the plan and specifications."*

Rev.George Seaman

On 16th February 1876, the trustees were asked to attend the next quarterly meeting to consider the plans. In March, steps were taken, as follows:- *"that we accept the plan submitted to the trustees of Grimston new Chapel that we invite tenders for building same - that Mr Lift be invited to lay the memorial stone - and that Mr Seaman give the address - sometime in May."* Tenders were advertised in the local press and plans and specifications were available to prospective builders in the no.1 vestry of London Road Chapel.

The New Chapel contract was decided at a meeting on 9th April 1876, when members agreed, *"that the contract for Grimston Chapel be given to Mr Leach for £345 on condition that matters can be satisfactorily agreed upon between Messrs Seaman and Lift and Mr Leach." It was planned "that Grimstone foundation services be held May 29th."*

Following which, at the June Quarterly Meeting it was agreed *"that the Grimstone new chapel be opened on the 24th & 25th September - by Mr Seaman and Mr Lift - Mr Cripps to preach on the Monday afternoon."* The new Chapel had 260 sittings and 200 adherents. In the late summer it was agreed, *"that the choice of new lamps for Grimstone new Chapel be left to Messrs Seaman and Lift."*

At the September quarterly meeting it was resolved *"that we advise the members of Grimstone new Chapel to entertain the question of selling the cottages, if an offer of purchase turn up - the matter to be left in Mr Seaman's hands."* It was also decided to insure Grimston Chapel for £200 and the cottages for £50 in the Connexional Office.

At the meeting on 8th November 1876, it was resolved *"that Mr Seaman and Mr Lift have liberty to make the best bargain they can in disposing of the old Chapel at Grimstone."* Later it was minuted, *"that we record our approval of the sale of Grimstone old Chapel, by Mr Lift to Mr Isaac Rudd for £40, and that Mr Lift consult Mr Nurse as to conveyance."*

In March 1878, Messrs Lift and Seaman were asked to see to the palisading of the Chapel. Later that year, the same two people were asked, *"to settle with Mr Baker for carrying out the work."*

The cottages remained as part of the trust property. In 1882, despite an earlier request to sell, the meeting resolved, *"that we do not give sanction to the Grimstone trustees to sell the cottages in connexion with the Chapel."* On 4th

December 1893, however, it was agreed *"that this meeting sanctions the sale of the cottages belonging to our trust estate at Grimstone and authorises the necessary steps to affect the sale and transfer the proceeds of the sale to be applied to the reduction of the debt on the Chapel."*

The meeting of 4th June 1894, declared *"that the report of the sale of the Grimston cottages and the reduction of the Chapel debt by £50 be received as satisfactory."*

In 1903, the decision to base the second Minister at Grimston was made, and in 1905 a committee was formed to search for a house for the Minister.

Appointed to the Chapel Committee on 1st June 1908, were:- William Collison, John J Worrell, Ernest Grey, Alfred Seaman, Jonathan Twite, William Foreman, Alice Watson and Herbert Hanslip.

A new trust was formed on 5th December 1910(4).

At the June Meeting in 1911 it was agreed, *"that the Circuit Rally and Reception Service be held on 19th July at Grimston. The afternoon service to take the form of a Camp Meeting, the Superintending Minister to preside, and the two new Ministers to speak."* At the evening meeting:- Chairman, Mr J Goodson, speakers Messrs Hunter, Twite, Hammond, Rasberry, Moore, Lincoln.

The P.M. Sunday School consisted of 9 teachers and 80 scholars in 1865 and 11 teachers and 78 scholars in March 1871. Alfred Seaman was the Sunday School secretary in 1897. Miss Collison held this position in 1898 as did Mr J Twite in 1899.

In 1900, there were 11 teachers and 81 scholars. Average attendances were 43 in the morning and 67 in the afternoon. Nine of the children were aged over 14 years.

Temperance. In 1900 a Juvenile Band of Hope had 61 members.

A New Sunday School was approved at the 1913 March Quarterly Meeting. In July 1913, the Rev. H Semper inaugurated a solemn service for laying the foundation stone of the new Sunday School. Stones were laid by Mr W Collison, (on behalf of the Sunday School), Mrs Watson and Mrs E Grey. An address was given by the Rev. Semper who said *"that owing to the growth in the number of members and children it was imperative that a school was built, and they were present to see one started and to ask God's blessing on their work."* A public tea was served to over 100 people, after which a public meeting was held and addresses given by the Revs H Semper, H.H Woodward and W.M Batterbee, and Messrs Barnett and W Collison. Mr H Sheldon was Chairman and Mrs Walter Collison organist. Proceeds amounted to £29.6.6½. The new School was officially opened in 1914.

The reception of the new Minister, the Rev A Banham, was planned to take place at Grimston on 15th July 1914 with afternoon tea at 5pm, Mission at 7 and public meeting at 7.30.

A Centenary Festival was held in 1976.

Membership Grimston P.M. - Pott Row

1900 - 34	1940 - 42	1975 - 27
1905 - 33	1945 - 38	1980 - 27
1912 - 53	1950 - 48	1985 - 23
1920 - 45	1955 - 35	1990 - 22
1925 - 38	1960 - 43	1996 - 20
1933 - 37	1965 -40	
1935 - 40	1970 - 31	

Grimston Society Stewards from 1933 Ex - Wes.

W Taylor, G Taylor, C.W Wittred, J Seaman, R Bartrum, Mrs D Barlow, Mr H Rumbles.

Grimston Pott Row Society Stewards from 1926

W Bunting, D Horsley, W Collison, W Hanslip, A.D Twite, C Bartrum, R Hanslip, S.J Watts, Mrs M Twite, P Prior, Mrs A.D Twite, C.H Worrell.

Notes:
(1)Wesleyan Trustees appointed on 28th March, 1876, were:- Stephen Roye labourer, John Jackson manuf. agent, William Thompson the elder, William L Armes manuf. agent, Robert Whitehead baker, Alfred Jermyn draper, Henry Gamble grocer, James Richardson Cozens hatter, Edward Eggett coal merchant, Robert Bush baker, Thomas Ashby Jackson manuf. agent, Thomas Merry school-master, Jonathan Paul shipowner, James W Groom grocer, Daniel Barnard fish agent, Edward Curson Bridges coal merchant, Jonathan Ashton Hillam stonemason.
(2)Grimstone P.M class in 1838 were:- John Collinson P&L, Rebecca Warner, James English, Maria Watts, Sarah Watts, William Smith, William Sayer, Ann Collinson, James Balding, Elizabeth Balding, Charles Adams, John Salmon.
(3)The 1875 P.M Trust Members were:- William Bunting senior, William Bunting junior, Dennis Horsley, Thomas Worrell, William Medlock, George Pointer, John Goodson, George Winkfield, Edward Baker, William Back,Lewis Pinchen.
(4)Members of the 1910 P.M trust were:- William Collison bricklayer, Jonathan William Twite carrier, Isaac Elsegood labourer, Charles Hazel blacksmith, Ernest Grey grocer, Herbert Hanslip platelayer, Alfred Seaman shoemaker, William Lake platelayer, John Thomas Worrell carpenter, Alice Watson widow/farmer, Abraham Boldero labourer, Walter Collison bricklayer, John Jude farm foreman, John Coe licensed hawker.

Chapter nine

HIGHGATE

The Wesleyan Methodists in Highgate were included with Lynn between 1837-1843 period, with no further information available.

The Primitive Methodist Plan of 17th June 1844, decreed *"that a Sacrament be given at Highgate," and on 16th June 1845, "that there be Anniversary Services for North End and Highgate."*

Highgate Chapel
(Photo Brian Hart)

On June 14th 1847, the Committee agreed *"that the Highgate House be offered to Brother Bullman at 1/- per week."* In March 1848, it was planned that Highgate have two preachers each Sunday during the next quarter. A month later, the Committee agreed, *"that the Highgate friends be allowed to have preaching in the afternoon at Mr Munsby's house by one of the preachers that's planned till next quarter day."*

A class was formed on 12th May 1848 with Brother Street as Leader, and an Anniversary was planned in October. The Circuit Authorities decided in September 1851, *"that Brother Burrell be requested to give notice to the party at Highgate to leave the house and offer it to Miss Smith and she be appointed to lead the class and Brother Key be assistant leader."*

George Cozens, a victualler of the Norfolk Temperance Hotel, sold a Chapel in Highgate on 3rd April 1852, to six men who were to be the Trustees of a Primitive Methodist Chapel(1). The Chapel had been built by Robert Mott in 1850 and sold to George Cozens in 1851. Hillen wrote that the Chapel was consecrated in November 1850 and let to the Wesleyan Reformers at £7.10.0 per annum(2).

The Highgate Chapel cost £101.4.0½ - total debt at completion was £60. The Society had 8 members. The Chapel could accommodate 120 people - 80 in rail-back seats and 40 in free sittings. Around 45-50 people attended the principal Sabbath services and 25-30 hearers attended the weekday services. A Sabbath School was taught in the Chapel and £3.0.0 per year rent paid. Pew rent collected in the past year was £1.11.0.

In May 1862, Mr Lincoln was requested *"to procure a supply for Highgate Chapel and a doorkeeper, etc."* Just over a month later, the June meeting agreed *"that the rails be removed from Highgate Chapel and Mr Gunton to be allowed to build the corners up to remove the nuisance."*

At the March 1863 meeting, Brothers J Barker, J Winch, R Dodman, senr, and R Dodman, were given permission to speak. The June meeting of the same year gave approval for Brother J Smith to speak in public and to go with Brother Harrison.

A week's Revival services were planned during the second week of the Lynn Mart, commencing 23rd February 1864. On 14th March 1864, Brother G Manning was given liberty to speak in public.

The Mart was given as the reason for a week's protracted meetings in 1865. In December of the same year, it was agreed *"that Mr Cook be Chapel Keeper at Highgate, in the place of Mr Dodman, resigned."*

In 1869, the Connexional Insurance Office insured the Chapel for £50, and Brother Suiter was employed to repair and clean the premises. In the following year it was agreed *"that Mr Watson have the cleaning of the Chapel at Highgate for about 5/- per quarter,"* and Brother W Neave was appointed assistant leader to Brother Ballard in the Highgate class.

Disruption to Sunday Services led to the following minute:- *"that 100 bills be printed for Highgate Chapel informing the inhabitants that, as we have been disturbed by children during Divine Service, we shall prosecute any offender of the kind in future. That the bills be placed upon the Chapel shutters and up at some of the shop windows, and one to be given to the constable and one to the Highgate police."* It was also agreed *"that the time at Highgate be altered from 6 to half past six o'clock on Sabbath evenings."*

In 1879, a harmonium was purchased, with a result that a year later it was agreed, *"that the Highgate singers have permission to hold a service of song, the proceeds of which to be devoted to the purchase of books."* The Highgate singers became a choir in 1881, and were told *"that they have liberty to hold their entertainment in the Chapel at Highgate next Thursday."*

The Chapel was rebuilt in 1883 and new trustees were appointed on 3rd September 1900(3).

Total Income in 1900 was £15.0.8 which included £1.12.6 pew rents, 15/- School rent, and £1.2.2 Anniversary collection.

Sunday School. On 1st October 1845, Brother Bulman was appointed superintendent to the Highgate school with Brother Catton, assistant superintendent. The Committee decided in September 1846, *"that we let the Highgate school to Margaret Smith at the rental of -/3d per week, with the understanding that it be liable to increase."*

A Committee Meeting held 2nd March 1863, resolved *"that as the Corporation refuse to allow the Gaywood children to be included with those of the Borough on March 10th, we recommend the Highgate School Teachers to give their children a dinner in Highgate chapel and for that purpose to raise a public subscription."*

In November 1864, The Sabbath School was allowed to hold a tea meeting for the school's benefit; tickets cost 8d, and a public meeting followed. In 1865 there were 15 teachers and 70 scholars and Brother T Beaman was appointed assistant superintendent.

Highgate was named 'Providence Chapel' in the 1868 report of

Sabbath Schools in the station. In 1871 it had 20 teachers and 60 scholars.

A decree of 14th August 1872, allowed *"that Highgate schoolteachers have liberty to give the children a treat provided they do not ask people for monetary aid."*

In 1873, Providence Chapel reported 29 teachers and 136 scholars. The name of Highgate reappeared in 1875, when 45 teachers and 153 scholars were recorded. In 1898, J Mitchley was named as Sunday School secretary.

In 1900, there were 9 teachers and 56 scholars, 3 of whom were over 14 years of age. Average attendance was 50.

Society Stewards from 1879 included:- N Ballard, G Eagling, J Mitchley, J Greenfield, R Dodman, D Dodman, H Smith, H Light, E Isbell, A Brighton, Mrs Green, Mrs Isbell, Miss M Green, C.J Mallett.

Membership

1900 - 34	1933 - 16	1960 - 14
1905 - 34	1935 - 17	1970 - 09
1912 - 37	1940 - 10	1975 - 07
1915 - 32	1945 - 07	1980 - 05
1920 - 21	1950 - 20	1985 - 05
1925 - 27	1955 - 15	1990 - 08
1929 - 26	1960 - 14	1996 - 09

Notes:-
(1)The 1852 Trustees were:- Benjamin Watson broker, Thomas Lincoln general dealer, Robert Lane porter, Howard Daisley painter, Richard Bone cordwainer, James Wilkerson shoe maker.
(2)History of Lynn: J.H Hillen. Vol. 2. p.649.
(3)The Trustees appointed on September 3rd 1900 were:- Frederick Head, James Jordan, George Hammond, James Henry Martin, Joseph T Mitchley, Charles Skerry, Frederick Palmer, Joseph Greenfield, George E Hipkin, David Dodman, Henry Riches, Frederick Whitby.

Chapter ten

LONDON ROAD

The First Chapel was built in 1826 when William Green Bellham was the Superintendent Minister. It cost £205 and could seat 350 people. It was opened on 2nd July 1826. Constructional alterations including the installation of a gallery, allowed seating for 530. In 1859 it was used for a Sunday School at a rent of £9.10.0 per annum.

Rev.W.G Bellham

Items from minute books

The singers and music were much discussed and contentious items in early meetings, as follows:-

1846. *"That the singers be at peace among themselves and no imorality brought against them, we do not consider it necessary to prohibit the use of music upon our singing gallery."* Later that year, *"That the three Mr L...'s be not aloud in the singing gallery on account of insulting Mr G Winkfield in the passage on Sunday."*

1847. *"That no musick be allowed in our singing galleries. That the persons who occupy the singing gallery be interrogated about the taking away of Mr Thorns seat."*

1848. *"That a meeting be convened on Wednesday night to investigate into the evil reports about Mr M... walking about with Miss L..."* Later, *"That as there is so much talk about Mr M... and Miss L...'s walking about together we think it commendable that they should both keep off the singing gallery for three months."*

"That James Sheldrick takes the lead of the singing in Lynn Chapel from this day (23rd August) and that he has no appointments on plan."

1851. *"That Mr Sheldrick see Mr H... to inform him that he is not to sit in the singing gallery."*

The accounts book in the 1850's showed the following:- one years water rate 2/6d, insurance for year 13/6d, winter quarter gas bill 18/8d, also, all per quarter:- paving rate 6/-, caretaker £1, window cleaning 2/- and poor rate 12/-.

The Present Chapel in London Road was built in 1859 at a cost of £1643.15.3½ (1). The total debt when finished was £871.7.10½. There were 220 members when built. Sittings were 620 in pews and 230 in free seats. On average, 800 people attended principle Sabbath services and 200 on weekdays.

1859. *"That Bro Lincoln procure the matts and matting for the Chapel. That Bro Lift keep the licence of the new Chapel. That no person that shall hire a pew in the new Chapel shall on any account, relet any seat therein. That Mr Stimpson make a new platform if the price be agreeable to trustees. That Mr Howchin be requested to give a detail of the way the pews, and sittings, are to be let. That the pews below in the body of the Chapel shall be let as follows: From the pulpit first pew -/6d, 2nd -/9d, 3rd 1/- and all the rest up to the door shall be 1/6 per seat. That no pews be let to two families for less than the regular price.*

That a bill be printed with a reward of one pound reward offered for the damage to the fence of Chapel.

That there be eight pendants below with two burners. That there be nine pillars in the gallery with one burner each and lacquered. That Bro Pank be requested to give an estimate of the cost of staining the back top and ends of seats varnishing. That Mr Howchin see Mr Hillam and Stimpson about the pews and that they be parralal instead of alternate."

1860. (20th April) *"That the trustees offer Mr Munson seventy pounds for the back land, and building in a strait line with the old wall, or seven shillings per yard, and Mr Munson take the building down and clear it away." (28th April) "That the* *trustees offer Mr Munson 140£ for the whole of the land to the south front, and be allowed to pay 150£ and the buildings thereon."*

Singers in the new Chapel were appointed by Brother L Rowe and under the charge of Mr Bailey. Singers were:- Mrs Musk, Mrs Pank, Mrs Lake, Mrs Daisley, Mrs Docking, Mr and Mrs F and C Sampson, John Thurne junr, R Dodman, J Machin, Henry Parnell, Thomas Docking, and William Hillin. It was also specified *"That no more persons are to be added without the sanction of the circuit committee or quarterly meeting. That we cannot sanction them having any music to play during divine service and none of the singers must neglect their school duties to sing without the sanction of their superintendent."*

"That the trustees consider the chanting last Sunday night in the Chapel to be derogatory of Primitive Methodism and that G Lee inform Mr H... William P... and Samuel C... that they must not presume to do any more. That the singers be requested to sit below in the Chapel near the pulpit which will be one means to prevent unauthorised persons intruding among them."

1861. A public tea was held with tickets for sale on the day. The ladies were asked to number the trestle tables, to draw lots for the places and to make all necessary arrangements for the tea. This included making two stones of cake for one hundred persons(2).

Three vestries were built by Mr Stimpson for the sum of £142.13.0. It was agreed that at the end of the harvest, collecting cards and circulars be issued to cover at least one third of the cost of the Chapel vestries. On 31st July, Building Society terms for two shares or £96, was accepted.

The following arrangements were agreed at the November meeting concerning the vestries:- *"to number them 1,2,3, and to have two sets of fire irons, to have inside doors, Mr Stimpson make the doors and that the chapel door be canvas both sides."* Mr Pank was asked to grain the vestries while Mr Lincoln was asked to supply tables and two dozen chairs.

1862. Benevolent Society First 'Official' Meeting was minuted:- *"that* *there be a tea meeting on Wednesday 11th June for the sewing ladies and the Benevolent Ladies who visit and the public likewise at 8d each(3)."* Provision was made for 200 people.

1863. Officers appointed were:- George Lee superintendent, James Hilling and Robert Couldstone assistant supts. George H Burrell treasurer, Edward Daw secretary and Sister Clethero Leader of a London Road School Class.

1864. After the old Chapel was sold, the Sunday School moved to the new Chapel. Revival Services were held in the vestries during the first week of the Lynn Mart, commencing 15th February.

Unfermented wine was used at the Sacraments.

Mr W Lift presented a Communion Service to the Society.

1865. Brother George Hammond was appointed superintendent of the Sunday School.

1866. A collection was made for the Lynn Hospital.

Two family pews were built in the Chapel and a platform and Communion Rail erected. Mr Lift was asked to ascertain the difference in cost of a light ornamental baluster and mahogany rail, over those made of deal. Back rails were fixed to all the free seats and battened match beading along the walls. Mr Pank was asked to paint, stain and varnish, both inside and out. Two vestry doors were mended and two doors had new cloth on one side.

The Chapel closed Sundays, 26th August and 2nd September. It was minuted, *"that we accept the Albion Hall at 10/- per day to be used during the time our chapel is closed for the Sunday morning and evening services."*

Refurbishment planning continued in July and August:- *"that flat splines be put on the side pews to accommodate the seat holder and the family pews be made each a foot wider, or more if required. That the first free seat be taken away and a short peice be taken away. That seats be put on the front of each pew near the entrance of the vestries. That we have a small stand for the bible something like that in the Wesleyan Chapel. That the table now in use do for the present. That coco nut matting be laid down inside the Communion Rail for the present - but if Mr Lincoln get a suitable peice of felt, or other carpet, he bear this in mind. That Bros Lift, Gunns and Smith get the cushions that are required made. That a rail on which to set seats be put on the pews in the body of the Chapel."*

A month later, it was agreed *"that a suitable cloth be provided for the table within the Communion Rail - to correspond with the carpet and cushions. That the singers be allowed to sit within the Communion Rail, for the present."* Mr Gunns was asked to speak to the superintendent of the Sunday School asking him *"not to allow the children to come near or occupy the seats near the Communion Rail."* Mr Lift and Mr Lincoln were allowed to occupy the two new family pews at 10/- per quarter.

Rev. R Howchin

The need for a new Sunday School was debated by the Quarterly Committee who decided that they were not able to undertake any new building work at the present time.

In October, the meeting agreed *"that the amount paid to Mr and Mrs Winkfield for cleaning and lighting, etc the London Road Chapel and vestries, be reduced 10/- per quarter, - and that the treasurer duly inform them of the reduction, when the next quarters salary is paid."*

1868. The thanks of the Circuit Committee and trustees were presented to 'Mother' and to all the members of the sewing society. They were affectionately requested *"to continue their valuable services for the benefit of the sanctuary."*

Brother Lift was requested to see Mr Munson concerning the roof of the adjacent property encroaching on land belonging to the trustees and also *"to turn the water from the roof onto his own land or property."* The school were permitted to begin a library with £2 allocated for books.

1869. Brother Worth was asked to see Brothers Rowe and Bailey about *"any measure they may think well to suggest to promote the efficiency of the singing of the London Road Chapel."*

The sewing committee ladies were allowed to have a public sale of their stock in the schoolroom, because Mrs Sampson had to relinquish her position as 'Mother' of the meeting.

Mr Rous was asked to measure the wall of a Blacksmith's shop being built near the Chapel. He was to report back if he considered it a nuisance.

1870. A ruling was passed *"that only one fire be lighted for the sewing meeting."* **Praise was expressed for the Rev. R Howchin,** who had been obliged to seek retirement from the Ministry due to illness, as follows:- *"that in consideration of the Rev R Howchin's long standing in the connexion, the valuable service he has rendered to the Norwich District, the success with which his labours have been crowned in the conversion of sinners, his sound judgement, tact, and skill in the erection of chapels, especially the London Road Chapel which ranks among the best if not the very best in the District; we cannot allow him to retire without taking steps at once to raise a few pounds to be presented as a testimonial to him."*

Arrangements were made for a tablet to be put up on the south side of the pulpit in memory of the late Rev.J Oscroft.

1871. The school was allowed to meet in nos 2 and 3 vestries during the severest of the winter weather and have a fire.

It was decided to build a schoolroom in association with the Chapel; dimensions to be 60 feet long and 30 feet wide if ground conditions would allow, and 15 feet from the ground to the wallplate. A collecting box was placed in the school. Friends were invited to assist in ground clearing. Later, a stable was demolished and old timber sold.

Messrs Rowe and Hall were asked to improve the choir by training a dozen scholars of the London Road school to sing with the congregation - arrangements were made for them to sit on the front seat of the Chapel.

1872. A meeting in February decided *"that considering the singers are doing so well and giving satisfaction we cannot entertain the request for a harmonium in London Road Chapel."* In 1870, Brother J White was given permission *"to beg money for a new harmonium."* This resolution probably caused heart-searching among some members of the Committee, because a week later was minuted:- *"the matter of Brother White collecting for a harmonium stand over for the present."*

Mr Waller was appointed assistant seat steward to Mr Shawl. His duties included putting strangers into the pews on the north side of the Chapel below. Mrs White and Messrs Docking and Bailey did a similar service on the south side. Six hymnbooks, at 1/10d each, were purchased for the use of strangers in the gallery.

1873. There was a ground swell of opinion in favour of a harmonium in the Chapel. The trustees were recommended to commence a new schoolroom as early as possible in the Spring.

1874. It was agreed that a harmonium be put in the Chapel and the trustees were requested to head the donation paper with a subscription. A committee was formed with Brother Batterbee secretary and fund collectors were appointed.

1875. Plans and specifications were drawn up for the new schoolroom which it was agreed *"would be heated by gas not fireplaces."* Mr Hillam was architect and surveyor and Mr Dawes the builder, who was allowed until the end of February 1876 to complete the project.

1876. It was agreed that the school ante-room be furnished with forms, table and chairs.

1877. Miss Lift was asked to play the harmonium and Miss White to lead the singing and arrange a list of names for the choir.

1878. Mr Fayers quotation of £115 for Chapel improvements was accepted, these being:- scarlet coloured cloth for the doors; bronze gas fittings, with brackets, with three lights under the galleries to correspond with the others. The gallery ironwork to be painted gold and white. Mr Pank to paint the outside of the Chapel. Hot water to be supplied to vestries and schoolroom.

While the Chapel was closed, Sunday services were held in the Music Hall. The Chapel re-opened on 14th/15th April.

Organ & Gallery (Photo Brian Hart)

It was agreed that a memorial stone for Mr Howchin be placed in the Chapel.

A singing class was formed for the training of lads and it was agreed to obtain a harmonium for the Sunday School.

1881. The trustees were given liberty *"to put a warming apparatus into their chapel and raise the money."*

Further problems with the choir resulted in the following minutes:- *"that we are satisfied with Mr Hall as the choir master and resolved to uphold his authority as such," and "that we inform all members of the choir that they must submit to Mr Hall's ruling in all matters affecting the singing in public worship."* There were several applications to join the choir; not all were approved.

1887. A fire occurred in the Chapel in the early hours of Sunday 18th December. It was reported that little damage was done, either by the fire or the effects of water(4).

1888. New Organ Planned. Following the receipt of a letter from W Savage (Circuit Steward) and G.M Bridges, the Committee agreed that there would be *"best possible means to adopt in raising the funds required for the purchase of the new organ and alterations connected therewith."* A fund was started and £90 promised by 1890. An organ committee was formed consisting of six trustees and six members outside the trust, with power to purchase an organ and build a choir gallery. A binding condition imposed was that the total cost was not to exceed £500 and not one penny was to be added to the Chapel debt.

1892. The organ (cost £260) and the gallery (cost £240) were installed in July; the total cost reported as being exactly £500, of which all was raised. Mr Jasper Wright the organist, was a key figure in the selection of the organ.

1894. A brass tablet in memory of William Lift, was installed over his former pew, and a second tablet installed in memory of Brothers Lincoln, Daw and Winkfield.

1895. A memorial service was held after the June Quarterly Meeting and the tablets were unveiled. Collecting cards were issued to all the Societies and penny subscriptions were solicited.

Improvements were made to the Chapel lobby and four windows.

1896. New trustees were appointed on 2nd March(5). The Rev. John Smith, President of Conference and former Minister in Lynn, paid a visit. An open air mission was held at Baptist's yard and Windsor Road.

Events in the 20th Century

1900. The total income was £97.7.8 of which £73.4.0 came from pew rents.

1910. Mr James Uttin appointed Sunday School superintendent.

1912. Deaths were recorded of Brothers W.M Lock, a member for over 50 years, and W Chadwick, Society Steward for over 18 years.

1913. New trustees were appointed on 11th August(6). An appreciative letter was sent to Mrs H.W Woodward for the work she had done in connection with the training of London Road scholars for the Connexional Scripture Examination. Both she and the scholars were congratulated on the splendid success attained.

1916. A letter of sympathy was sent to Mr and Mrs Harris of King's Lynn, whose son was reported missing.

1925. New trustees were appointed on 4th March(7).

1927. The first Orange and Gift Sunday was held in the Chapel on 18th December. Over 1000 oranges, with nuts and apples, were distributed to needy people.

Orange & Gift day (Acknowledgements Messrs Jewsons)

1953. A Bazaar was held on 2nd December. The Chairman was Lord Fermoy and the event opened by Mrs Reed of Downham Market.

1955. "St.James Old Time Fair" was held on the open space at the back of the Chapel. Admission was 6d, children 3d. Teas were 1/6d. There was a concert in the schoolroom from 6.30-7.30pm. A Circuit Rally was held on 26th October and the speaker was Mrs Lincoln Ralphs.

1959. St. James Centenary Services

On Tuesday 31st March, the preacher was Rev. J. Eric Thorpe, supported by Rev. Hubert J Martin, Chairman of the District. Supper in the schoolroom cost 4/-. Anniversary services were held at 11am and 6.30pm on Sunday 5th April. Preacher was Rev. W Oliver Phillipson. Services were conducted by Rev. Ernest Partner.

1979. New Church Hall

The old School Hall was demolished and a modern Church Hall constructed. Architects were Maurice Whalley and Partners of Lowestoft and builders Wagg and Jex of King's Lynn. On 21st November, the door was unlocked by George Clitheroe, the Church's oldest member, and a commemorative plaque unveiled by Paul Bartlett Lang of the Joseph Rank Benevolent Trust. A service of dedication was conducted by Rev. Geoffrey Thackray Eddy, Chairman of the District. The sale of London Road South, grants, a bequest and money raised locally made a total of £45,030.

L/Road Church Hall(Photo Brian Hart)

Society Stewards from 1879-1996 included:- N Ballard, W Bailey, G.M Bridges, W Chadwick, G.H Curtis, A Fackney, C Thompson, E Whiley, A Freeman, W.C Baker, H Burman, K Hooke, J.W Nicholas, G.F Merrywest, V.W Faulke, G Baker, K Neal, R.J Charlesworth, J.R Mindham, E.H Garfoot,

R.S Hamon, A.G Cornthwaite, Miss J Ayton, J Lake, N Panton, Mrs E Dyble, J Woodcock, L Elflett, Mrs L Evans, Dr A Chase, B Hart.

Membership 1900-1996

1900 - 313	1925 - 195	1950 - 202	1975 - 153
1905 - 296	1933 - 179	1955 - 147	1980 - 166
1912 - 207	1935 - 159	1960 - 136	1985 - 140
1915 - 177	1940 - 137	1965 - 176	1990 - 143
1920 - 160	1945 - 175	1970 - 159	1996 - 118

Ladies Concert at L/Road c.1925

Notes:-
(1)Disbursements were:- To R Munson Esq. £350.0.0. To Bill for Jenne gas fittings £201.12.2½. To Mr Sharpe of Norwich £60.7.6. To Mr Stimpson, Builder £73.10.0. A Bill of Extras unpaid £58.5.7. Total £1643.15.3½.
(2)Costs were:- Bread 4/8d, Flour 2/6d, Tea £1.1.1½,(Mr Ballard's bill), 10lbs ham 6/4d, (Mr Lift), Stamp 11d.
(3)The Benevolent Society began, un-officially, in March 1862. The Quarterly Meeting approved the rules prepared by Wm. Lift. Messrs Lincoln and M Gibson were appointed treasurer and secretary. Over the years, the Society paid many visits to the sick and needy to provide cheer and a little practical help.
(4)Lynn News and County Press:24th December 1887. The fire was first noticed by two policemen on patrol, PS Smith and PC Jarvis at about 2.40am, who observed a glare through the windows of the Chapel. PC Jarvis ran to the police station and telephoned the borough surveyor and the buzzer was sounded immediately. Meanwhile, Mr Silcock was called at 2.52am and Mr Wootton was awakened at about the same time by Sgt Smith. At 3.0am Mr Silcock arrived at the scene of the fire and arranged for a hose reel to be brought from the Theatre, and, using a hydrant immediately opposite the Chapel, soon had a jet of water playing on the fire. The flames were extinguished before the steam fire engine and manual arrived. The Chapel keeper was called and lit the gas in the Chapel *"And the fire was then quite extinguished."* The cause of the fire was thought to be due to *"overheating of some flues belonging to the heating apparatus connected with the Chapel, as the floorboards in the neighbourhood appeared to have been the first to take fire in the southeast corner of the building."*

(5)New trustees appointed on 2nd March 1896 were:- Messrs William Savage, George Hammond, James Docking, William Sporne, John Goodson, James C Frost, Joseph Day, John Watson and Frances Youngs (continuing) and:- George M Bridges artist, William Chadwick engineer, Henry Coe grocer, James Coleman mechanic, Thomas S Cox foundryman, Ambrose Cutting machinist, William M Lock carman, Alfred W Maxey chemist, John Savage engineer, Walker E Taylor commercial traveller, all of Lynn, and William Pitcher gardener of Saddlebow. Chairman was Reverend Arthur J Wardle.

(6)New trustees appointed on 11th August 1913 were:- Messrs William Savage, John Goodson*, William Sporne*, John Watson, James C Frost*, Joseph Day, James Coleman*, Ambrose A Cutting and William Pitcher (continuing) and:- Claydon Dines coal merchant, Edward Denny fruiterer, Arthur Edward Michelson blacksmith, Robert Collison coal merchant, Henry Sheldon insurance superintendent, Charles Curtis* railway inspector, John Appleton* cooper, George Musson* assistant insurance superintendent, William Henry Wagg* shop manager, Lacey Edwin Harvey company manager, William John Burnell insurance superintendent.

(7)New trustees were appointed on 4th March 1925. (Continuing trustees* from above) New trustees were:- Messrs Joseph Poyser insurance superintendent L.P. William C Baker shop assistant L.P. James S Reeve civil servant, Alexander Fackey clerk, George Pickard fish merchant, Edward John Batup Oliver clerk L.P. William J Edwards shop manager L.P. George W Clithero engine turner, George Alcock insurance agent L.P. Henry Harris miller, James Uttin railway guard L.P. William Panton engine driver L.P.

Chapter eleven

NARBOROUGH

The Wesleyan Methodists. On the 19th April 1864, Mr Henry Boyce, a farmer, sold land in the village centre for £25 to twelve trustees for the building of a Chapel(1). In 1895, he sold an additional piece of land adjoining the Chapel, for £20, to Edward Eggett and others(2). New trusts were appointed in 1919 and 1920(3). There was a Sunday School library in existence during the 1880's which was evidence of the presence of young people.

Three wall plaques were installed in the Chapel in memory of members of the Boyce family.

Wesleyan Membership 1885-1930

1885 - 25 1890 - 16	1895 - 15 1900 - 08	1905 - 04 1910 - 04	1915 - 05 1920 - 04	1925 - 03 1930 - 05

The Primitive Methodist Circuit Meeting of 10th June 1878, decided *"that Swaffham Circuit officials be written to informing them that they have not held any services at Narborough for some time and ask them if they intend to give the place up."* At the same meeting it was agreed *"that the reply from Swaffham be left with Mr Seaman(the Superintendent Minister) as to*

Narborough Chapel (photo Brian Hart)

whether Narboro or Pentney shall be put on the plan."

On 9th September 1878, it was agreed *"that Narborough comes on the plan and that the services be planned for half past two and six."* In 1879, the name was removed from the plan.

Society Stewards 1933-1990:- F Nash, H Brown, Mrs D Callaby.

Combined Membership after 1932

1935 - 06	1950 - 09	1955 - 08	1970 - 13	1990 - 08
1940 - 07	1955 - 08	1960 - 07	1975 - 15	1996 - 09
1945 - 05	1960 - 07	1965 - 07	1980 - 10	

On 2nd March 1960, new trustees were appointed for the Chapel and school.

Notes:-
(1) The 1864 trustees were:- John Jackson manufacturer, Edward Holmes engineer, Edward Eggett grocer, Henry Johnson draper ,Thomas Merry school-master, Robert Whiteman baker, William Armes manufacturer, Thomas Ashby Jackson clerk, William Arnold cordwainer, Thomas Harrison Curson ship owner, William H Boyce farmer, William Johnson farmer.
The Superintendent Minister was Rev John Hearnshaw.
(2)The 1895 trustees included:- Edward Eggett coal merchant, Robert Whiteman gentleman, Thomas Ashby Jackson living in Lancashire, William Arnold clerk, Thomas Harrison Curson hosier, William Johnson farmer.
The Superintendent Minister was Rev John Appleby Barrow-Clough.
(3)The members of the 1919 trust were:- W Johnson, William Robert Smith, Alfred Jermyn, John J Petrie, Herbert Sutcliffe, Edward George Flowerday, James M Barrett, John W Harris, William T Wildbur, A.B Ketteringham, William T Hayes, B.W Jermyn.
The members of the 1920 trust were:- Hubert Alfred Jermyn, Hugh Robert Croot, Harold Verry, Charles Herbert Lemmon, Charles Golding Barrett, Harry Brown, Ernest Bridges, William Henry Scase, John Pilling, Henry Sheldon, Walter Howes, Alfred Claxton Dye, John Henry Dew.

Chapter twelve

NORTH END and NORTH LYNN

The Wesleyan Methodists obtained a base in Pilot Street, purchased from Geo Garner and William Hill on 12th and 13th November 1795. Preaching services were held in an 'orange house' in North End(1).

A Chapel built in North End (1862) was taken over by the Primitive Methodists. A new Chapel of 400 sittings was built in Pilot Street in 1883 at a cost of £1000. A trust was appointed on 29th September 1882(2).

The Primitive Methodists earliest available record is March 1838. Two classes were listed, one led by Cathrine Cushing (later removed to Yorkshire) with five members and five on trial, and the other by William Rounce, with 5 people on trial.

The Quarterday Meeting agreed on 6th December 1844, *"that Mr Merry have liberty to buy North Lynn Sunday School."* A week later, Mr Merry, and others, were given *"liberty to beg for North Lynn Sunday School."* A resolution of 1st October 1845, decided *"notice to lease the North End Schoolroom be given immediately."*

Brother Bullman was appointed assistant superintendent to Brother Suiter in February 1846 and in July it was agreed that the trustees enlarge the schoolroom. In 1848, Sister Lock and Jackson were asked to raise a juvenile class in the schoolroom.

A Chapel built in 1856 cost £200. It had 106 sittings and 20 adherents. Two freehold cottages were purchased for a schoolroom in 1861 for £75. Trustees were appointed on 29th January 1862(3).

In December 1862, it was resolved *"that the Committee kindly request the trustees of North End, to see that, someone, open the place, and light it, up, when there is preaching, and other meetings."*

In 1863, John Winch was appointed superintendent, Thomas Barker assistant supt, A Lock treasurer and Elizabeth Rowe secretary. John Winch and Thomas Barker were appointed as Leader and Assistant Leader of the class. Later that year the school was asked to pay the trustees £4 per annum rent.

The June Meeting in 1864 agreed *"that we make an effort at once to erect a schoolroom or Chapel at North End as it may be most expedient."* It was decided to hold a fisherman's tea on 5th September and the profits to be given to the schoolroom.

A piece of land fronting the property purchased in 1861, was bought from Mr J Langley for £15. Additional trustees were appointed and a deed was made(4). The District Building Committee was asked to give sanction *"to enlarge or improve or rebuild the North End Schoolroom."* It was also agreed to appoint Mr Kerridge as architect, for the old building to be pulled down and no fireplace built.

Estimates submitted by seven builders for the project (North End No.2) were above the sum the trustees had considered spending. This resulted in a new plan and specifications being prepared. In November 1864, it was agreed *"that Mr Scott be deputed to see Mr Stimpson and enquire if he is willing to complete the schoolroom at North End for the amount of his first contract,ie £136 and if so, he is at once engaged to do it, although we do not bind ourselves to commence the work forthwith."*

Miss A Lock again lent £10 (she had already lent £10 interest free) and was asked in June 1865 to be treasurer. The July meeting decided *"that an effort be made forthwith to erect a schoolroom at North End. That Mr Gunns, Lift and others have an interview with Mr Stimpson, (builder) and obtain the possible cost of the said schoolroom and get a specification and tender."* On 13th September it was decided *"that four feet be added to the intended schoolroom."* Also, *"that the trustees accept the tender of Mr Stimpson for building North End schoolroom provided he comply with the deputation appointed to wait upon him (Messrs Gunns, Lift and Lincoln) relative to vestry and privy."* Two weeks later it was agreed *"that Mr Stimpsons last tender (or statements) in reference to North End schoolroom be received and that he be requested to commence immediately."*

A Committee meeting in October decided *"that Mr Gunns and Mr Lift be requested to concur with the Builder as to the situation,etc. of the Petty for North End schoolroom."* also, *"that the foundation stone of North End schoolroom be laid this day three weeks, if arrangements can be made for this time, and that Mr Gunns preach on the occasion,"* and *"that Miss Lock be invited to lay the first stone of North End schoolroom."* The meeting also agreed *"that Mr Sharrat (Sailors' Missionary) be invited to attend the above services,"* and *"that there be a tea meeting, on the above occasion, that Miss Lock (and others) be requested to solicit trays."*

Later it was agreed that the new schoolroom be built on the old ground with two doors on the east side, Mr Sharrat to preach at the foundation stone laying, a tea meeting in the London Road vestries on behalf of North End and Mr Pank was asked to advise on quality of glass and sanction was given to solicit donations. Arrangements were made for a stone, bearing the inscription 'Primitive Methodist Schoolroom 1865,'to be placed on the building front. Mr Pank to give an estimate for installing gas.

The January 1866 Meeting agreed *"that £70 be paid to Mr Stimpson for North End school."*

In April members decided that the schoolroom be opened on May 13th by Mr Thoseby and that Mr Gunns preach on May 16th and a tea meeting afterwards; trays to be solicited, tickets 1/- each.

In August, Miss Lock was recommended *"to make enquiry what is paid by the Wesleyan people to their North End Chapel cleaner and we think they are not in a position to pay more than 10/- per quarter."* The Sunday School was recommended to hold their Anniversary Services on August 26th in the

Albion Hall.

In 1867 the Chapel was presented with the Communion Cups once belonging to London Road. In 1868, Mr Winkfield was asked to take care of school flags and banners. Mrs Dalgleish was given the use of the Chapel, free of charge, *"to raise a day school."*

In 1869, the schoolroom rent was fixed at £4 per annum and with *"the surplus of the North End school fund be devoted to reward books for the children."* Brother Pank was asked to examine the schoolroom and do any necessary repairs to piping and windows.

Fencing was erected in front of the schoolroom in 1871. Special services were held with collections for lighting, warming and cleaning the Chapel. In 1872, Brother Gunns was asked to see Mrs Allen *"and offer her 1/- per week to clean North End Chapel and if she can not we ask Mrs Thorne to take it."*

In 1879 Messrs Ballard, Gibson, Lift and Seaman, were asked to inspect the waste land belonging to North End property and report back to the committee. Following which, Mr Lift was instructed to sell a piece of land and *"that £12 be asked for it."* A month later the Committee decided *"that we do not consider it advisable to sell any part of the property."* On 16th December 1881, the Committee agreed *"that the North End property be bought for the Connexion and that we accept Bro Able's offer of £150 on mortgage on the above property."* It was also decided *"that the Circuit apply to the Building Committee for leave to buy the buildings at North End."*

The sale of North End Chapel was approved in July 1900 and Mr Wardle instructed to obtain sanction from the General Committee. In December it was decided *"to the letting of North End Chapel for a Sailors Mission Room at a rental of £20 per year subject to the conditions of trustees per agreement,"* and in March 1902, *"that the people now hiring North End Chapel are not prepared to pay rent of £20 per year, we take it back and work it as best as we can."* At the meeting of 9th April 1901, Miss Scott was asked *"if she will take charge of North End for 3 months and on what terms."* Three months later the Committee recorded *"that we heartily express our thanks to Miss Scott for the gratuitous service and successful service she has rendered to our North End Society during the last three months."*

New trustees were appointed in 1904(5). In 1920 the Committee agreed *"that an expression of our appreciation of the work of Mr and Mrs Green at North End be made."*

The Sabbath School Teachers' Plan showed the PM Sunday School had 120 scholars in 1849, 21 teachers and 100 scholars in 1865 and 4 teachers and 45 scholars in 1900. Average attendance was 30 and 5 children aged over 14. The school secretary in 1898 was C Dines followed by J.H Curtis in 1899.

The Move to North Lynn, was caused by two factors, ie, local people were being re-housed in the North Lynn Estate, and a planned new route to the Docks meant the demolition of the Pilot Street Chapel. Following permission by the authorities in 1951, a site for a new Chapel was purchased in 1952 at the junction of Losinga and St.Edmundsbury Roads.

After several years of deliberation by various Methodist committees, the Synod agreed in May 1962, to the new building. The architect was Mr Clifford Dann and the construction by Collison Builders. The stone laying ceremony occurred on Saturday 20th April 1963, being performed by Mr W Hunter-Rowe, a member of the East Anglian District Chapel Committee. Prayers were led by the Rev. John Garfoot, who became the Minister with pastoral responsibility for the Church, assisted by the Rev. Ernest Partner.

The Chapel could seat 70, with adjoining Sunday School hall, stage and further seating for 110, with a movable partition between Chapel and hall. Cost was £10,000 which the Borough Council paid, as equivalent reinstatement compensation. The opening ceremony was performed by Miss M Green on 30th November 1963. She claimed *"it was a shining light*

North Lynn Chapel (Photo Brian Hart)

to the community around it." The Rev. H.J Martin MA.BD. Chairman of the East Anglian District, preached the sermon.

The Pilot Street Chapel closed on 16th September, 1962. The Sunday School was held in St. Edmundsbury School until the new Chapel opened.

While the new Chapel was being built services were held at North Lynn Community Centre. Mr and Mrs Garfoot (parents of the Rev. John Garfoot) took an electric organ, which Mrs Garfoot played to accompany the singing. She continued as Chapel organist until aged 90. The Chapel was presented with "Hymns and Psalms" and "Good News" Bibles in memory of Mr and Mrs Garfoot.

PM Membership 1885-1932

1885 - 58 1890 - 64 1895 - 35	1900 - 23 1905 - 25 1910 - 41	1915 - 34 1920 - 20 1925 - 30	1930 - 32 1932 - 33

Membership after Union

1933 - 36 1935 - 28 1940 - 19 1945 - 23	1950 - 16 1955 - 09 1960 - 12 1965 - 27	1970 - 27 1975 - 21 1980 - 21 1985 - 24	1990 - 25 1996 - 22

PM Society Stewards 1879-1932:- Mrs Barnes, T Barker, A Back, Mrs Fisher, G Boldero.

Society Stewards 1933-1990:-E Wilson, H Jacob, J.W Pyshorn, Miss Lyon, E.J Lake, Miss M Green, W.R Petchey, J Barber.

Special Event. A Service was taken by George Thomas (who became Lord Tonypandy) the Speaker of the House of Commons.

Notes:-
(1)Mr Robert Bush (1910).
(2)The 1882 Wesleyan trustees were:- William Thompson the elder timber merchant, William L Armes manufacturer's agent, Jonathan Jackson manufacturer's agent, Alfred Jermyn draper , Jonathan Paul shipowner, Robert Whiteman baker , James Regester tailor, Thomas Ashby Jackson factor, Robert Bush baker, Augustus Fredk Curson solicitor's clerk, Arthur Jonathan Scott merchant's clerk, William Thompson (junior), Fredk Ollett merchant's clerk, W Jackson grocer, Chas Herbert Lemmon banker's clerk, Thomas Merry school-master, Edward Eggett coal merchant, William Johnson farmer - Terrington St.Clement.
(3)The Primitive Methodist trustees in 1862 were:- Brothers Robert Dodman mariner, James Judd grocer, Laurance Hayes, George Henry Burrell, Martin Gibson shoemaker, William Lane and Abraham Claxton shoemaker of Wolferton.
(4)Additional P.M trust members in 1864 were:- Brothers W Lift butcher, T Lincoln hardwareman, Edwd Pank plumber, B Harrison, H Judd miller of West Winch, J Winch and T Barker fisherman.
(5)Primitive Methodist trustees in 1904 were:- Thomas Barker fisherman (continuing), Claydon Dines coal merchant, Arthur J Williamson labourer, John Runnells labourer, Bullen Curson clothier, Arthur Back engine driver, James R Fox butcher, Geo D Thorsley builder and Willoughby G Wilkinson mechanic. Chairman was Rev. Geo Bell.

Chapter thirteen

SOUTH WOOTTON

The Wesleyan Methodists have no available record of their presence in South Wootton. (North Wootton was credited with 5 members in 1837).

The Primitive Methodists carried out preaching in Mr Lewis Pinchen's house, in a room specially prepared by the Society. At a Circuit Meeting on 14th July 1858, it was agreed *"that we send a note to Mr Pinchen of Wootton to thank him for opening his house for preaching in such circumstances - being turned out of doors."*

Mr Hill was given liberty to speak in public, on 16th March 1863. In May it was decided *"that the friends at Wootton have a tea meeting on Whit Monday on behalf of their preaching room furniture."* In August 1866, members agreed *"that a sympathetic notice to Mr and Mrs Pinchen of Wootton, expressive of our determination to do all we can to support the Wootton Society and we request the members residing both at Wootton and Rising continue their membership as heretofore."* The following year in March it was resolved *"that a candle collection be appointed at Wootton early next plan."*

Efforts were made to buy land for a Chapel in 1868, as follows:- *"that Mr Gunns and Mr Lift wait on Mr B... as soon as possible requesting a piece of ground for a Connexional Chapel."* This venture failed, but in June 1874, Mr Pinchen was asked to attend the next Quarterday Meeting and provide any relevant information with regard to having a new Chapel at Wootton. Two weeks later, *"that Messrs Gunns, Lift, Ballard and Pinchen wait authorized to arrange buying a piece of land for a new Chapel at Wootton and that they wait upon Mr Adams on Wednesday for that purpose."* Two days later the Committee agreed *"that the purchase of land at Wootton by Messrs H Gunns, W Lift, N Ballard and L Pinchen be considered perfectly satisfactory."*

Mr N Ballard was appointed treasurer and trustees were appointed on 9th September 1874(1).

The plan for the Chapel was accepted by the Committee on 22nd September 1875. The contract to build was secured by Messrs Dye & Clack for the sum of £115 and Mr Hillam was requested to survey the work. Arrangements were made for the memorial stone to be laid on Wednesday 3rd November by Mr Lift; for Rev. Seaman to preach, for 100 bills to be printed and for tickets to be 9d at the stone laying.

South Wootton (Photo Brian Hart)

On 10th November, it was decided *"that Wootton Chapel be covered with slates instead of tiles"* and *"that Mr Ballard pay the first instalment for Wootton Chapel on receipt of a note from the architect."*

An agreement was signed on 24th November 1875, between Henry Adams gamekeeper, and George Seaman, Superintendent P.M. Minister, for a piece of land measuring approximately 10 yards by 7 yards, with hedges and outbuildings, for the sum of £17. It was bounded by the public road to the Common and land owned by Henry Adams and Mr Bloomfield.

South Wootton Chapel had 100 sittings and 50 adherents. The cost was £150.

Messrs Ballard and Pinchen were asked to *"attend to making the road to Wootton Chapel"* in February 1876. It was also decided *"that the front and the side next to the gardens by Wootton Chapel be fenced by post-palings etc."*

In 1878, the Circuit Committee decreed *"that we do not see our way to give consent to the Wootton friends to have the music at their religious services."*

New trustees were appointed in 1898(2).

The PM Sunday School was started in 1877. By 1900 there were 4 teachers and 28 scholars; average attendance was 20, of whom 10 were over 14 years. William Lake was appointed Sunday School secretary in 1897.

Temperance. There were 24 children in the Band of Hope and 16 adult total abstainers in 1900.

Society Stewards from 1879 included:- L Pinchen, W Lake, Chas Grice, C Porter, E Isbell, F Medlock, H Southgate.

Membership

1900 - 08	1925 - 12	1950 - 09	1975 - 16
1905 - 10	1933 - 11	1955 - 05	1980 - 14
1912 - 12	1935 - 14	1960 - 06	1985 - 14
1915 - 21	1940 - 09	1965 - 14	1990 - 21
1920 - 16	1945 - 09	1970 - 15	1996 - 25

New trustees were appointed in December 1931(3). A Camp Meeting was held on 1st July 1934, and the preachers were Messrs W Bland, H Fendley, S Marshall and Reynolds.

An additional piece of land was obtained in 1962, being a gift of H.D.J Southgate. This enabled the building of a Church hall and kitchen extension. A Movable partition was placed between the Hall and the Chapel. New trustees were appointed in 1964.

Notes:-
(1)Trustees appointed in 1874 were:- Lewis Pinchen dealer, William Youngman shepherd, Thomas Rudd blacksmith, John Grice labourer, William Gamble farm bailiff, Benjamin Rains labourer, Samuel Lake farm bailiff, James Rains labourer, Henry Rawson shepherd,(all of Wootton) and Nathaniel Ballard butcher, Lynn.

(2)Trustees appointed in 1898 were:- J.O Rains, William Youngman, Benjamin Rains, Samuel Lake, Henry Ransome, (continuing) William Lake platelayer, South Wootton, Charles Grice platelayer South Wootton, William Overson labourer, North Wootton, Robert Hipkins labourer, Wolferton, Anthony Hopkins dairyman, Gaywood. Chairman was Rev Arthur J Wardle.
(3)Trustees appointed in 1931 were:- Anthony Proctor, Charles Grice, William Lake, Charles Porter, Fred G Medlock, George Bunkall, Mrs Lilian Bunkall, Percy Oates, Alfred Arnold and John Howard Grey.

Chapter fourteen

TERRINGTON ST CLEMENT

The Wesleyan Methodists had a Society of 66 members in 1837 that, except for 1838, increased as follows:-

1837	1838	1839	1840	1841	1842	1843
66	63	69	79	83	88	90

There were six class leaders in 1837:- Wm Johnson (19), Wm Slaite(15), Thos Nicholls(11), Hen Winterton(8) Mr Reader(7) and Fras Jewson(6).

Society Stewards were Mr Bates (1838), Mrs Ward (1840) and W Hand (1843).

The First Chapel was built when, on 16th December 1813, a piece of copyhold land 30' x 21', was purchased from Mr John Ward by Maxmillian Wilson, Preacher of the Gospel, and five trustees(1). A Sunday School started in 1830 and met in the Chapel.

Wesley Chapel(Photo Brian Hart)

The Second Chapel was planned and, by a deed of the 9th April 1844, James Mills, builder and carpenter of Terrington St. Clement, sold 2 roods and 32 perches of copyhold land at Kidd's Corner, also known as Kidd's Cross, to fourteen Wesleyan Methodists for £80. (He had bought it for £70 a year earlier). It is recorded that the Chapel was built by Mr Mills for under £600(2). The foundation stones were laid in July and the Chapel dedicated with a service on 29th October 1844. James Mills became a Chapel trustee. An organ was installed in 1875 and a rostrum built in 1883. The Chapel was reseated in 1893. The Chapels were enfranchised in 1863 and 1876 by indentures from Lord of the Manor, George William Pierrepont Bentinck. New trustees were appointed in 1877(3).

The Schoolroom(Photo Brian Hart)

The New Schoolroom was necessary because of the thriving numbers, ie 30 officers and teachers and 260 children. Bricks from the old Chapel were used in the foundations. Stones were laid by Mrs M Johnson and Mr W Ward on 27th May 1885. It was built by Mr Mountseer of Terrington for the sum of £315.12.0. The original building was 30'x50'. A classroom was added in 1895, and further classrooms installed after the first world war.

The Burial Ground. A Trustee Meeting was held at Terrington on 3rd December 1879. Present were:- Rev. W Allen Chairman, and Messrs J Jackson, Ward, Armes, Wm Johnson, Jermyn, R Croot and J Ellis. Among the items resolved were:- *"that 50 feet of meadow land be railed off with iron hurdles - keeping 12ft at least for roadway. That a gate be opened near the end of the meadow not taken in for its use, and that the present gateway be used for the burial ground. That the graves be prepared East and West, and to be commenced at the West side of the cemetery - except when site is purchased. That a central path be made about 4ft wide."*

An adjourned meeting was held on 9th December at Tower Street vestry. The main items resolved were:- *"that all the Trustees residing in Terrington act as the Interment Committee and that the burial ground shall be for the use of the Members and Seat-holders of the Wesleyan Methodist Church and Congregation worshipping in Terrington, and that any exceptional case shall be decided by the majority of the Interment Committee - and any difficult case to be decided by all the Trustees(4)."*

It was also agreed, *"That 10/6 for each grave be charged for permission to select a spot for burial, and that no restriction be made as to place, except that the graves left to the choice of the Interment Committee shall be opened two deep on the North and South sides."* The first burial occurred on 12th February 1880 and burials officially ceased in 1982. There are approximately 574 plots.

Information from Plans. Messrs W Johnson and Jos B Ash were preachers in 1887. Messrs W.S Carter and J Ellis were Society Stewards in 1918. There were 9 Class Leaders, 123 adult members and 40 junior members. Local Preachers included H Croot and T Croot. In 1930, the Society Stewards were Messrs W.S Carter and R.H Kerkham. There were 11 Class Leaders, 110 adult members and 37 junior members.

The Primitive Methodists had a Society of 13 members in 1836, who paid 9/7½d quartering. In 1838 there were 5 members + 10 on trial(5). Written in the March Column of the Rolls was the following:- *"this place is broken up and the place left off the plan, partly thro neglect of local Prs and partly thro disunion among themselves."* In 1844 the Society had increased to 19 and Messrs Reeve and Wharfe were Leaders and Lay Preachers. In the September, the Circuit Committee agreed *"that a revival meeting be held at Terrington and a Travelling Preacher."* In the September of 1845, it was decided *"that Terrington Chapel be continued by making a collection once a quarter."* Brothers Howchin and Lowe were requested to see Revd. Chambers (The Wesleyan Minister) *"to solicit the loan of the old Terrington Chapel to hold our*

Missionary Meeting." A Camp Meeting was planned during 1847 and 1849. On 13th July 1849, the Society were given permission to buy land for a Chapel and to collect for the same. Brothers Lincoln and Briggs were asked to be trustees. The Circuit Committee received the following memorandum in September.

September 7th 1849
Lynn Quarter Day
Dear Brethren,

May peace be multiplico. This is to inform you that we have received the estimate for the chapel and cottage.

Land	£25
Title deed	£7
Lime and bricks	£15
Bricklayers and woodwork	£72
Windows and frames	£10
Slateing	£10
Total	£137.10

And we believe we can raise £30 and that we request a tea meeting 4th October and two travelling preachers afterwards.

Yours respectively
The Trustees

In June 1850, the Society were asked to build directly and Mr Langham asked to obtain the sanction of the Building Committee.

The Chapel in Popes Lane was built in 1850 at a cost of £149.4.11$^{1}/_{2}$. There were 22 members when the Chapel was built which was capable of accommodating 136 people (96 in pews & 40 in free seats). On average, 100 people attended services on Sundays and 50 on weekdays. Pew rents for twelve months realised £4.16.0.

Two iron bar stays were installed for wall security and a *"new and elegant"* chandelier purchased. Ten perch of spare land was rented for 5/- per annum, for future enlargement of the Chapel.

Within a decade a new Chapel was being planned, as indicated by the following minute at a meeting on 9th May 1860:- *"that Mr Howchin to canvas for donations at Terrington for new Chapel on Monday the 24th day of June next."* Later that year, Mr Rowe was requested to revise the new Chapel plan, and the Committee recommended the trustees *"in the event of either altering their Chapel or pull it down."* On 17th September, the Committee agreed *"that the Terrington friends have their new Chapel stone be laid on Friday 28th and at first the opening services Mr Lowe, Bond and Beckerlegge, and Mr Wigner on the second Sunday any additional be left to the plan maker."*

The New Chapel built in 1860 was freehold with accommodation for 200 sittings with 100 adherents. The cost was £350. Mr Burrell held a note of hand for £100; this was called in and the money was advanced by Mrs May Billing of Lynn, who held a bond for the same amount signed by George Reeve, Robert Wharfe, William Bennett, Benjamin Alexander and Thomas Lincoln.

Liberty to speak was given to Brothers Gent, Simpson and J Studd (1861), R Webster (1863), W Wharfe (1864), H Weston (1864). In 1862 it was decided *"that Brother Bennett of Terrington have no appointments next quarter, being disabled through advanced age."*

The Society made a successful application, in 1870, to build a vestry and stable in their Chapel yard.

George Reeve was written to asking him *"whether his way be clear to come into the Ministry."* (He died in Canada as the Rev. George Jacob Reeve, on 24th November 1879, aged 28 years. A commemorative plaque was installed at Terrington Chapel).

George Daws and Henry Briggs were given liberty to speak in 1871. The Society were authorised to put up a plain tablet in their Chapel to the memory of Brothers B Gent, J Everett and W Wharfe on 18th March 1872. In the same year, the Sunday School were asked to pay £2 rent to the Chapel.

Permission was requested to renovate the Chapel in 1878 and Mr Hillam was asked to see about the alterations. However, the Circuit Committee decided that *"the matter of altering the vestry had better stand over."*

The alterations were eventually sanctioned *"on condition the Society raises one half of the cash."* The alterations were carried out by Willis and Son and Mr Seaman was planned to re-open the Chapel in May 1879. A year later, the Committee were pleased to record *"that the Terrington Chapel alteration ac/- be received as very satisfactory."*

Brothers James Cooper and William Walker were given liberty to speak in 1881. The Society were allowed to put up a tablet in the Chapel to the memory of Mr Robert Wharfe on 11th June 1900. R Eggleton, G Reeve and D Laws were given notes of liberty in 1910 and a Rally was planned in 1913. On 4th December 1916, the Circuit Committee agreed *"that a letter of condolence be sent to Mr and Mrs Creasy, Terrington, who have lost a son on the battlefield."*

Brother W Crawford and Mrs Howling were appointed Class Leaders of Terrington Christian Endeavour on 3rd June 1918. Application was made to the Building Committee in 1919 to allow the trustees to spend £100 on their Chapel property.

The Committee agreed on 21st June 1921, *"that Miss Collison be congratulated re the success attained by her in the training of pupil teachers and that mention be made of our appreciation of the benefit derived by our School at Terrington."*

Permission was given for the Society to form a new class on 6th March 1922, and Miss Pratt was appointed Leader.

The PM Sunday School had 10 teachers and 55 scholars in 1865. In 1871, 11 teachers and 65 scholars. W Pratt was appointed secretary in 1897. In 1900 there were 9 teachers and 57 scholars - average attendance was 40 and 2 children were over the age of 14 years.

Temperance. In 1900, 50 children and four adults were registered as total abstainers.

PM Society Stewards 1879-1958 included:-

R Wharfe, Mr Shepherd, R Creasy, R.W Wharfe, F Coulson, R Eggleton,

B Creasy, W Pratt, J Reeve, W Bland, J Skeels, Mrs Parker, H Mason, W Delamore, W.H Barnes, A Bland.

The Chapel in Popes Lane closed in 1958 and the Society worshipped at the former Wesley Chapel.

Society Stewards (former Wesley) from 1933:-

W.S Carter, R.H Kerkham, W.E Brown, R Croot, N Clarke, B.C Scales, G Reeve, Miss V Clarke, J Ward, W.C Hill, Mrs M Durrant, T Lake, E Hunter, D.W Durrant, Miss M.A Reeve, A Bull, J Skerritt, W.H Kerkham, C Bartrum, N Robinson, A Pepper, Mrs A.J Hatton.

Special Events

The Chapel Centenary (Wesley) took place in 1944. A 'Final Effort' - sale and entertainment, was at 6pm on 25th October. Thanksgiving Sunday was held on 29th October and a Special Service 'The start of the Second One Hundred' was held on 5th November - Rev F.A Farley, M.A. BD(London). A Circuit Rally held on 19th March 1947 and Rev F.W Loy of Leicester, was planned to visit. The Emmanuel Choir from London gave a concert in 1967. A range of celebrations took place to mark the Schoolroom Centenary in 1985.

Membership 1933-1956 - Popes Lane Chapel

1933 - 24 1935 - 24	1940 - 28 1945 - 21	1950 - 19 1956 - 13	

Membership from 1933 - Wesley Chapel

1933 - 97 1935 - 88 1940 - 92 1945 - 89	1950 - 79 1954 - 92 1956 - 89 1961 - 87	1965 - 73 1971 - 82 1975 - 77 1980 - 63	1985 - 60 1990 - 66 1996 - 45

The Methodist New Connexion

A Chapel existed in the last Century and was on the site of the Oddfellows' Hall.

Ministers residing in Terrington

Pastor J.B Ritchie	1915-1921	Rev Henry Snell	1922
Rev J.A Wells	1925	Rev Gordon Read	1926
Rev Charles Oyston	1930	Rev C.E Brian Cowburn	1934
Rev A.J Ward	1937	Rev H.G Rolls	1940
Rev W.H Robinson	1943	Rev G.B Middleton	1946
Rev E Harrap	1950	Rev F Leslie Henry	1951
Rev James L Cooper	1956	Rev David Caink	1961
Rev G Leonard Hodson	1966	Rev H Adrian Smith	1970
Rev Frank E Sykes	1975	Rev Robert A Richards	1981
Rev David Blacklock	1986	Rev Barbara Savage.	1993

Notes:-
1)The 1813 trustees were:- Thomas Broadbent of King's Lynn, George Easton of Terrington, Francis Jewson of Terrington, farmer, Thomas Nichols of Terrington , farmer and Thomas Ayre of King's Lynn, ship owner.
(2)Terrington St. Clement Methodist Church, Schoolroom Centenary Booklet 1985: Rev. R.A Richards BA.
(3) Trustees appointed in 1877 were:- Henry Bates farmer of Terrington, George Cooper gentleman, of King's Lynn, Matthew Johnson gentleman, James Neve gentleman, William Ward farmer, all of King's Lynn, Thomas Bowers, John Cobb and William Johnson, farmers, Robert Croot cattle dealer, Henry Briggs the younger, blacksmith, John Ellis grocer and draper, all of Terrington, John Jackson, William Linay Armes, manufacturers; William Thompson timber merchant, Alfred Jermyn draper and Robert Bush confectioner, all of King's Lynn.
(4)The Trustees residing in Terrington were:- Messrs H Bates, M Johnson, W Ward snr, Wm Johnson, T Bowers, J Cobb, R Croot, H Briggs junr, J Ellis.
(5)PM Membership Rolls 1838-1844. The five members were:- William Read, Leader and Preacher, Henrietta Read, Matthew Seeking, Jacob Alexander and William Bennett. Those on trial were:- Mary Come, Robert Reade, Mr Bowers, Mr Bunkle, Mrs Taylor, Mr Weston, Susan Carter, Elizabeth Clarke and Stephen Carter.

Chapter fifteen

WEST LYNN

The Wesleyan Methodists earliest available records show that a Society was present in 1837 and for the next six years membership remained fairly constant, as follows:-

1837 16	1838 16	1839 14	1840 17	1841 17	1842 14	1843 17

Mr Broadbent was Society Steward in 1838 and also the Wesleyan Circuit Steward. A Chapel was built in 1870, following conveyance of land from James Vincent on 21st February 1870. It could accommodate 130 people. Trustees were appointed on 25th February 1870(1). A Certificate of Worship was received on 15th June. At the turn of the Century, the Chapel was refurbished with the ceiling, dado and pulpit made from finest pitch pine. Electric lighting and heating were installed c.1928. A Certificate of Marriage was issued on 25th February 1935.

West Lynn(Photo Brian Hart)

On 27th June 1964, two stained glass windows in the east end of the Chapel, were dedicated in memory of members of the Allen family. Mr Josiah Allen was superintendent of the Sunday School for over 50 years and a Society Steward for about the same time.

On 21st May 1922, there was a conveyance of land from Mr A.H Boswell. A new brick schoolroom was built by Warren Bros. and opened on 15th November 1968. This replaced one made from corrugated iron and wood.

Society Stewards included:- J Allen, W Ellis, Mrs Allen, A Baron, D Cornwell, B Allen, Mrs F.M Allen, Mr Young, S Benstead, L Allen.

Membership

1885 - 15	1920 - 22	1950 - 30	1980 - 30
1890 - 15	1925 - 21	1955 - 33	1985 - 29
1900 - 22	1930 - 19	1960 - 29	1990 - 33
1905 - 20	1930 - 24	1965 - 32	1996 - 20
1910 - 21	1940 - 24	1970 - 38	
1915 - 12	1945 - 22	1975 - 38	

New trustees were appointed in 1920(2), 1943(3) and 1966.

The Primitive Methodists earliest available records show 22 members in December 1836. The names of a Society of 9 (8 members + 1 on trial) are recorded in 1838(4). Between 1836 and 1845, membership varied between 28 and 7. In the 1st quarter of 1846 there were no members shown but a collection of 3/6d was recorded.

There was a Sunday School and Mr Howchin (the superintendent) was *"affectionately requested to assist at the West Lynn School Anniversary"* on 21st September 1845. On 12th November 1845, the meeting agreed *"that West Lynn School be allowed to have a tea meeting."*

With no members in the 1st quarter of 1846, it was decided *"that West Lynn be re-missioned next Quarter by local preachers on the Sunday morning and evening."* That this was unsuccessful is evident by the decision taken at the next Quarterday Meeting in June, namely *"that West Lynn come off the plan."* A Quarterday Meeting on 16th December 1850 decided *"that we try to obtain a house for preaching at West Lynn and that it come on the plan and two preachers be appointed."*

In March of 1851 it was agreed *"that the T Preachers enquire as to the probability of getting a Chapel at West Lynn."* At the June Meeting *"that West Lynn be missioned by two preachers."*

West Lynn came on the plan for an afternoon service only in December 1862 and was allowed preaching in the evening in March

West Lynn Sunday School c.1935

1863, but in the September was taken off the plan again. In March of the next year, it was agreed *"that West Lynn come on the plan with two services"* and *"that we give sanction for West Lynn friends to commence a class and that the preachers appointed be requested to lead it for the next quarter."*

Three old forms were lent to the Society for six months. In June 1864, members agreed *"that there be a school opening at West Lynn by Mr Lincoln"* and *"that the West Lynn friends be allowed to collect for the furnishing of the house for preaching and supply the school with books."* A meeting in October resolved *"that the case of West Lynn be brought forward next Committee Meeting."* The following matters were agreed one week later:- *"that a letter be written to West Lynn informing the friends there that certain persons have agreed to assist in paying the rent of the preachers house to the quarterday. That Mr Lincoln be appointed to visit West Lynn on Sunday week to make arrangements if possible for the future welfare and existence of the cause.* In December, Brother G Winkfield was asked *"to go to West Lynn and fetch the forms belonging to the Society also the books lately used by the school."* (The books were subsequently lent to East Winch). On 2nd July 1879, It was agreed *"that a new class be formed at West Lynn."* There is no further information.

Notes:-
(1)Trustees in 1870 were:- William L Armes manufacturers Agent, Thomas A Jackson manufacturer's agent, Robert Bush baker, George Croot merchant, Edward Eggett coal merchant, Thos Kirton Ellis carpenter, William Johnson farmer of Terrington, Edward T Markham Auctioneer, George Moore yeoman, Robert Rands butcher, William Thompson senior, Joseph Vincent.
(2)Trustees appointed in 1920 were:- Alfred Jermyn, William Robert Smith, William Allen Ellis, Hubert Alfred Jermyn, Hugh Robert Croot, Joseph Allen, James Ernest Mann, John Pilling, James Morgan Barrett, Charles Golding Barrett, Edward George Flowerday, John Henry Dew, Herbert George Howard, Bertram William Jermyn, Walter Howes, William Bennett Paige, Ernest William Ellis, Charles Jarvis, Harold Verry, William Samuel Carter.
(3)Trustees appointed in 1943 were:- Harold Verrey, Josiah Allen, Edward George Flowerday, Reginald Joe Allen, Florence Maud Allen, Reginald George Read, Herbert Stanley Allen, Ruby Florence Mann, Bernard Martin Allen, Leslie Lloyd Allen, Eveline Holmes Butt, Edmund Alexander Wilson and Albert Curry.
(4)PM Circuit Rolls 1838-1844. In 1838 the Society was:- Jonathan Haws, Leader, Sarah Haws, William Tolladay, Robert Cudbeth, Frances Woods, Mrs Cruit, Pheby Tolladay, Mary A Neal and Mr Cunningham (on trial).

Chapter sixteen

WIGGENHALL ST GERMANS

The Wesleyan Methodists had 30 members in 1837, divided into three classes Mrs Starling (10), Sam Evans (11), Robt. Scott (9). The Society increased membership as follows:-

1837 30	1838 35	1839 48	1840 55	1841 53	1842 58	1843 60

Mr Beckett was the Society Steward in 1838 and the Class Leaders were 'Starlings', 'Scott' and 'Evans'. In 1840 Thos Beckett was named Society Steward. On 9th November 1863, Chapel trustees were appointed(1). In 1873 Wiggenhall St. Germans was listed as having a Wesleyan Chapel with 145 seats. This was a rented building on a 99 year lease from 25th March 1811.

St.German's Chapel(Brian Hart)

Land was purchased on 1st June 1897, from Mr Michael Starling and a new Wesleyan Chapel and Schoolroom built in 1900 at a cost of £880. A Registration for Worship Certificate was received on 1st January 1901 and a Registration for Marriage Certificate on 1st March 1902. A new Chapel was needed as the existing rented building was dilapidated and unsuitable and the lease expired in 1910. There were 31 members in 1900 and, on average, 100 regular hearers.

The Primitive Methodist Society was listed in the 1844-45 Plan, with a Revival Meeting on 10th November, with Brother's Jackson, Sheldrick, Guymer and Woffen planned as the Preachers. A meeting on 17th July 1844, agreed *"that sermons preached at St. Germans for benefit of the Chapel."* The Circuit Meeting on 11th March 1850, resolved *"that St. German's Chapel be bought at £115 provided it can be obtained and we pay the conveyance."*

The Primitive Methodist Chapel was bought freehold in 1850 for £122.18.0. James Langham was superintendent and there were 22 members. Total debt after completion was £111.0.0. It had 105 seats - 90 in pews, 15 free sittings. On average 100 people attended Sabbath Services and 40 hearers on weekdays. A Sabbath School paid 10/- annual rent. Trustees were appointed(2). Mr Lift was mortgagee for £80.

On 10th June 1850, it was resolved *"that this meeting agrees to use their influence by encouraging and urging the trustees of St. Germans Chapel to pay off the debt, £5 per annum till it is reduced to £80.0.0 for the first four years."* In September 1850, members agreed *"that the Sunday School be properly and exclusively a PM Sunday School at Germans."* It was also decided *"that the Friends at Germans be told that they did wrong to allow the Chapel for a controversial lecture and that they do so no more."* Resolutions included:- *"that the teachers of Lynn be requested to go occasionally to Germans,"* and *"that the T.Prs inform the Leaders and Chapel Stewards that the rule prohibits misuse of Chapels."* Purchasing Services were arranged on 3rd November 1850, with Mr Cooper preaching in the morning and Mr Johnson afternoon and evening.

In 1864, the trustees were urged to pay ten pounds off the Chapel debt and Brother Thomas Smith was approved as a Prayer Leader. An October 1869 meeting resolved *"that we sanction the application from St. Germans to put a board floor in the Chapel provided they raise according to promise the amount required."*

On 16th December 1872, Brother Dent was appointed leader of the

Wednesday Class with Brother Hilton assistant.

Approval was given in 1881 to raise the money for improving and fencing the Chapel. At the June Quarterly Meeting, it was resolved *"that we apply for the sanction of the District Building Committee to materially alter St. Germans Chapel adding not more than 20£ of the expenditure to the present debt."* The meeting of 12th March 1882, agreed *"that steps be taken to form a new trust for St. German's Chapel"* and the Society was given sanction *"to beg for a harmonium."* Brother Buck was appointed treasurer of the Sunday School in June 1882.

In May 1908, five people were allowed to have collecting cards *"for the purpose of collecting for new organ fund(3)."* Messrs P George, F Lewis, S.J Dane and F King were appointed as the Chapel Committee on 7th March 1910.

PM Membership

1900 31	1905 30	1910 21	1915 18	1920 21	1925 25	1930 19

Membership after Union

1935 14	1940 10	1945 08	1950 03	1955 06	1960 14	1965 12
1970 14	1975 12	1980 13	1985 09	1990 05	1996 05	

Following Union, the two Societies agreed to worship together and the services were held in the ex Wesleyan Chapel. The former PM Chapel, which was in St. Peter's Road, was sold to Mr Harry Brown in 1933.

PM Society Stewards 1872-1932. W Claydon, Mrs Wardle, S Kew, F Fuller, R Howes, Mr Ostler, P George, J Elmer, S.J Dane, W.S Lewis, F King.

Society Stewards from 1933. E Emms, S Craig, J.H Lawson,

Mrs A Whittrick, Mrs J Lawson, Mrs R Whittrick, Mrs F.M Barber, Mrs P Plaice, Mrs H Porter.

Sunday School. The PM Sunday School had 15 teachers and 60 scholars in 1865 and 12 teachers and 78 scholars in 1871. Miss Elmer was the secretary in 1897 and W Lewis in 1899. In 1900, there were 9 teachers and 81 scholars with average attendance of 54; one scholar was over the age of 14 years.

Temperance. In 1900, a Band of Hope had 27 juvenile abstainers.

Notes:-

(1)Wesleyan trustees appointed on 9th November 1863 were:- John Jackson manufacturer's agent, Edward Holmes surveyor, Edward Eggett coal merchant, H Johnson draper, Robert Whiteman baker, G Clarke, M Starling, David Westland blacksmith, William Henry Boyce farmer.

(2)Primitive Methodist trustees were:- William Bridges, James Kidd, Watson Hastings, Richard Claydon, Robert Bradfield, Thomas Lincoln, George H Burrell, John Carter and George Offord.

(3)The five people collecting for the organ fund were:- Mrs Wardle, Miss Groom (elected treasurer) Miss Hilton, Miss E Bales, Mr H Howard.

Chapter seventeen

WIGGENHALL ST. MARY the VIRGIN

The Wesleyan Methodists earliest available reference is Michaelmas 1837 when St. Mary's were credited with 5 members. After falling to 4, this total reached 7 in 1843.

The Primitive Methodists had 15 members in 1845 and were on the Plan to be re-missioned(1). A Lovefeast was scheduled for Sunday 2nd August 1846. On 15th March 1847, it was agreed *"that there be a tea meeting at St. Mary's next plan when one of the travelling preachers are present to assist the finances of the chapel."* In December 1848, it was resolved *"that Mr Ward and Burrell collect for St. Mary's Chapel,"* and in January 1849, *"that we give notice to leave St. Mary's Chapel to get a house to preach."*

There were 10 members in 1848. On 17th February 1849, the Reverend Ward was asked *"to see Mr Merry and trustees of Mary's Chapel and about settling the money due, among themselves, in five parts."* The March meeting in 1849 agreed *"that we give Mr Buffham a shilling a quarter for the Chapel and he take the seat rents."* In September 1850, it was decided *"that an anniversary be at Mary's and a proposal to Mr Buffham to rent the Chapel to trustees for £4 a year."* A Chapel anniversary and Revival Meeting were scheduled on 13th October 1850, with Brothers Johnson, White, Coe and Stanham preaching. Another Revival Meeting on 28th April 1850, had Brothers Reeve, Wharf and White as preachers. In June 1851, a sermon and tea meeting was held for the benefit of the Sunday School. A Camp Meeting was held on 31st August 1856, with Preachers W Wainwright, T Lincoln, G Winkfield and M Gibson.

The March meeting of 1858 agreed *"that the affair of St. Mary's Chapel be left with Mr Howchin and Mr Britain, and they inform Mr Buffham, that we accept the*

Chapel on hire, at 4£ per year with the understanding that he return 10/- per year for a pew and that he be allowed to collect out-standing debts for himself and our hire commence at Sunday Aug. next."

On 15th October 1862, it was agreed *"that Bro Scott and Coe be deputed to wait on Mr Buffham of St. Marys to see if he will sell the Chapel, and if so the terms he will come to in disposing of it."* The May 1864 meeting decided *"that the arrangements for the purchase and settlement of St. Mary's Chapel be left in the hands of Mr Scott."* One month later, on 13th June it was agreed *"that a tea meeting be held at St. Mary's or two if necessary to raise funds for the purchase of the Chapel."*

The new St. Mary's Chapel c.1910

On 5th May 1865, an agreement was reached between the executor of the late Mr John Buffham and the trustees for the sale of land and Chapel for £60, thus making it Connexional property(2). The sum of £50 was borrowed on note of hand from Mr R Wharfe of Terrington. Thomas Buffham was the Steward. In December it was decided *"that only essential repairs be done to St. Mary's Chapel at present, and that general repairs be attended to early in the Spring."* In March 1866, it was agreed *"that the trustees of St. Mary's Chapel be allowed to take steps to repair their property."*

Protracted negotiations lasting several years, took place between the Circuit Committee and Gustavus Helsham, owner of St. Mary's hall, who wished to obtain the Chapel as his property. He offered a new site for the Chapel. The Committee agreed, subject to certain conditions. However, he failed to meet the requirements of the Circuit's solicitor regarding an abstract of title. Mr Helsham then offered to buy the Chapel for £60, but this was declined as being insufficient to build a Chapel on another site.

The class leader in June 1866, was Mr F Dent. In 1867 Mr Rawlings was appointed leader and Mrs Whiteman, assistant leader.

In 1868, a dispute resulted in the following minute:- *"that Mr B... be informed that he is opposing Primitive Methodist law and usage when he states that a woman has no right to officiate as Class Leader and by so doing has caused a disturbance and thereby hindered the Cause of God."*

The trustees were recommended in June 1869, *"to take action at once in regard to the proposed improvements and alterations needed in that Chapel."* Money was borrowed on notes of hand, as follows:- £40 from Mrs Gunton a widow of Magdalen, £10 from Mr William Alt of Lynn, and £5 from Mr R Hammond of Magdalen. (A total of £55 at 5% p.a.) This enabled repairs to be carried out. Finances were never healthy, for example, in October 1873, it was decided *"that in the opinion of this Committee the trust funds of St. Mary's Chapel, is not in a state, to warrant the advance of any money for lamps at present as there is 2=15=0 due for interest, and cleaning and only about 2=16=1 in hand."*

The January 1875 Committee decided *"that the architect prepare the plan for new seats and board floor for St. Mary's Chapel."* Later it was agreed *"that St. Mary's Friends be allowed to put their tea off till after harvest."* The Society had a tea meeting on Tuesday 5th December 1876, *"to raise money to pay for lamps, etc."*

An increased offer to £80 in 1877, by Mr Helsham for the Chapel, was left in the hands of Messrs Seaman and Lift with the Committee agreeing *"it is our opinion that £90 should be received by us for the matter."* Finances were again in a parlous state and the June meeting of 1880, agreed *"that the Mary's deficient Chapel a/c be paid out of the general Chapel fund."* Brothers Thomas Buffham and Haythorpe were given permission to speak in December 1881.

New trustees were appointed on 21st May 1891(3). A trust meeting was held on 29th August 1893 with Messrs Daw, Savage, Youngs and J Smith (Chairman) who reported *"that he and Mr Hillam had been that day to examine the Chapel and found it in a most sorry plight."* It was decided to recommend the Quarterly Meeting *"that the best course would be to sell the Chapel on condition that another site be secured for a Chapel so as not to close the door altogether against future efforts in the village. Failing in this course the Chapel should be repaired and secured against the weather and all efforts be made to pay off the debt*

St. Mary's Sunday School Anniversary 1921

which including the £10 now due for interest amounts to £60." The Quarterly Meeting in September agreed and in June, the next year, the Committee agreed *"that the report of the reduction in liabilities on St. Mary's Chapel by £40 be received as satisfactory."* In December, it was decided *"that Mr Wardle and Mr Pointer make enquiries as what is best to be done with the Chapel at St. Mary's."*

The 1885 March meeting agreed, *"that the question of repairing, renovating and reopening St. Mary's Chapel be relegated to the Ct Committee."* This resulted in the trustees being recommended to renovate the Chapel. The Reverend Wardle was given a free hand as to how the money was obtained. After a break of three years, services recommenced in 1896.

The Society was given permission in 1902 to collect money to clear their debt of £20. New trustees were appointed on 7th March 1904(4). In 1908 the trustees discussed building a new Chapel on the site of the old one, and a proposal to do so was passed in September 1909. Discussions between Rev. W.E Walmsley and Mr John Stubley, the owner of St. Mary's Hall, ended with a decision to build a new place of worship as proposed. Mr Stubley was Mayor of Batley in Yorkshire and a generous benefactor.

The balance in hand was £3.16.2 and efforts to raise the money for the building programme were started immediately. By 1910 the balance had risen to £415.15.7.

The New Chapel. On 29th October 1909, an agreement took place between Mr John Merrison and Mr William Pepper, on behalf of the trustees, and Robert Eggleton, the builder, to erect a Chapel and Schoolroom on the site of the existing Chapel, according to plan and specifications prepared by Mr J.M Kerridge of Wisbech, for the sum of £336.0.0 inclusive of seats to platform only. The builder agreed to commence work immediately, to enable the foundation stones to be laid on the 29th November and to complete the work before the 30th January 1910. A penalty clause in the agreement imposed a fine of 10/- per day on the builder for every day beyond that date until the building was completed. Bad weather or strikes relieved the builder of this liability. The Chapel, was completed by the agreed date with accommodation for 100 sittings and 80 adherents.

Messrs Stubley junr, J.R Merrison, Arthur Pepper, Thomas Harrison and Phillip George were appointed to form the Chapel Committee on 7th March 1910.

Special Events. Circuit Rallies held in 1912 and 1913. A visit by the the President of Conference on 22nd October 1918. A camp meeting on 14th August 1921, commenced at 10.45am, with T Moore, J.W Twite, R.J Seaman, H Scase and A Askew. The Society Stewards secured a meadow, a waggon for speakers and an organ, prior to the Sunday.

New trustees were appointed on 1st December 1931(5).

The PM Sunday School started after 1846. There were 12 teachers and 49 scholars in 1865 but in 1871 only 4 teachers and 20 scholars. In 1897, J Merrison was the secretary, followed by Wm Merrison in 1899. In 1900, there were 7 teachers and 30 scholars. The average attendance was 25. There were 7 children over 14 years. The Sunday School Anniversaries were great occasions and around 1900, were held in a marquee erected in a field adjacent to the Chapel. An accounts book produces interesting statistics(6).

Temperance. There was a juvenile Band of Hope in 1900.

Society Stewards from 1879:- T Buffham, J Buffham, R Tuck, J Dunmore, J Buck, S Mincher, D Long, S Kew, Mrs Beales, G Ostler, D Laws, J Edwards, R Calton, J Merrison, W Pepper, A Cox, T Harrison, J.W Calton, Mrs Calton, G Coldham, G Coe, F Ham, Mrs M Ham, J Dennis.

Membership 1900-1996

1900 - 08	1925 - 14	1950 - 11	1975 - 06
1905 - 15	1933 - 13	1955 - 07	1980 - 15
1912 - 09	1935 - 12	1960 - 08	1985 - 13
1915 - 09	1940 - 14	1965 - 12	1990 - 12
1920 - 15	1945 - 14	1970 - 08	1996 - 11

New trustees were appointed in September 1962.

A well-equipped kitchen was added in 1978 by first levelling an old yard at the back of the Chapel and building on this. The members (supervised by professional help) also built new toilet facilities and electrically rewired the entire premises. In 1982, it was discovered that a large area of the Chapel and Schoolroom were infested with dry-rot.

Repairs were carried out at a cost of less than £2,000 (one estimate had been £10,000).

Notes:-

(1)The members of St. Mary's Society were:- John Stanham,(L&LP), John Buffham, Thos Cowling, Sarah Gell, James Gell, John Swaby, Eliza Howe, Maria Whiteman, Maria Ann Cowling, John Germany, Elizabeth Towler, Mary Catton, Samuel Neeve, Mary Neeve.

St. Mary's Crockery

(2)The trustees of 5th May 1865, were:- John Whiteman butcher, Jonathan Scott P.M. Minister, Thomas Buffham labourer, Charles Haythorpe labourer, James Wardle labourer, Frederick Dent labourer, John Buffham farmer, Robert Hammond shopkeeper, James Gunton shoemaker, William Seaman labourer.

(3)The 1891 trustees were:- Chas E Taylor grocer, William Savage cashier, William E Daw butcher, George Pointer dealer, Francis Youngs coal merchant (All of Lynn). William Hunter of Pentney, carrier, John Overton of Terrington, miller. David Baxter of West Winch.

(4)The 1904 trustees(all of St. Mary's) were :- John Merrison farmer, William Pepper steward, John Dunmore labourer, William F Thorpe labourer, William Dunmore labourer, William Watts labourer, Frederick Buck sluice keeper.

(5)The 1931 trustees were:- James Joshua Stubley mill owner, Richard Allen horseman, Richard John Hall labourer, George Coldham labourer, Edwin Arthur Rudland labourer, Herbert John Caswell smallholder, John William Calton* foreman, Ralph Burman fruit grower, Charles Lewis carpenter, Charles Rogers Lewis carpenter, George Henry Coe labourer, John Robert Carter labourer.

(6)**Hire of Marquee - £2.5.0. Brass Band - £2.0.0. Meat - £3.2.8. 400 Oranges - £1.3.6. 10lbs Butter - 15/10. One gallon Milk - 1/4. 10½lbs Ham - £1.1.0.**

***Mr John Calton** became Sunday School Superintendent in 1919 and this was the beginning of a remarkable record of service by the Calton family. Mr Calton remained the Superintendent until his death in 1964 (he had also served as Chapel and Society Stewards); his place was taken by his daughter, Marion (Mrs F Ham) who filled that office until about 1990. He also performed the duties of Chapel Treasurer for many years until this duty was taken over by Marion from 1958 - 1961. His wife, Mrs J Calton, was organist for 50 years until her death in 1969 when her daughter Marion became the organist and remained so until her death in 1991.

Chapter eighteen

HARPLEY & BLACKBOROUGH END

HARPLEY

The Wesleyan Methodists were in the Swaffham Circuit but little is known of them. The Gospel Hall was built c.1870 and the Worship Certificate dates from 5th June 1874. The property was sold in 1952.

The Primitive Methodists earliest available record shows 41 members in December 1836. Up to 1848, membership ranged between 33 and 68. There were three mixed classes in March 1838:- 1st Class - Mary Forster (20 members + 3 on trial), 2nd Class - George Rudd (18 members + 1 on trial), 3rd Class - John Porter (14 members + 2 on trial). C Porter was given permission to speak in 1851.

A Chapel was rented from Mr Forster of Harpley in 1863 at £6 per annum. Mrs Forster and Mr Richard Wright let the seats. (Mr M Beavis replaced Mr Wright in 1864).

An agreement was made between Mr Forster and Rev T.W Rous on the 11th October 1870, for the purchase of two cottages for £150, as a site on which to build a Connexional Chapel. (The land measured 32ft in length and 24ft in width). The Chapel was built in 1871 by Mr Bolding for £350. A memorial stone was laid by William Lift and opening Services planned for 26th November. The Committee specified *"that the windows be glazed with plain obscure glass. That there be a family pew on each side of the rostrum as large as the space will allow and that the Chapel be cladded instead of 'ceiled.'"*

Brother T Rudd came on plan as a local preacher in 1872. In 1880, the Circuit Committee recorded the following minute:- *"that having heard that some unknown brother of this meeting has offered £50 free of interest for the Harpley Chapel, providing three others can be found who are willing to do the same, We request Mr Smith to do his best to seek for three who will join his unknown brother in this noble object."* Mr Smith was also given liberty *"to open a subscription list on behalf of Harpley Chapel."*

The repair and renovation of the Chapel was approved in 1893. The Chapel re-opening was planned for 15th and 22nd April with a tea and public meeting on the 23rd. In June, the Circuit Committee were pleased to hear *"that the report of the renovation of Harpley Chapel at a cost of 44£ and showing that the whole amount has been raised and the bills paid be received as satisfactory."*

New trustees were appointed on 6th June 1898(1) and 22nd February 1911(2). A Circuit rally, planned in 1913, realised £1.18.0.

A letter of condolence was sent to Mr and Mrs Arter in 1916, expressing sympathy on the death of their son on the battlefield.

In 1900 the total income of the Chapel was £42.17.4 of which £8.4.9 came from pew rents.

The Sunday School was first mentioned in 1844. In 1846, there were 7 teachers and 35 scholars. In 1865 6 teachers and 24 scholars and 8 teachers and 50 scholars in 1871. There were 9 teachers and 90 scholars in 1900 - average attendance was 79 and 20 scholars were over 14 years old. Mr E Pilgrim was secretary in 1897, followed by Mr A Mace in 1899.

Temperance. In 1900 there were adult and junior Bands of Hope, with 35 adults and 33 juniors registered as abstainers.

Society Stewards from 1879 included:- R Lewis, R Haws, G Hawes, R Hammond, W Clarke, T Hammond, J Hammond, F.L Fake, A Lake, J Lake, C.T Mountain.

Membership

1900 - 43 1905 - 38 1912 - 48 1915 - 45 1920 - 40	1925 - 31 1933 - 41 1935 - 37 1940 - 30 1945 - 25	1950 - 28 1955 - 26 1960 - 22 1965 - 22 1970 - 18	1975 - 17 1980 - 13 1985 - 11 1990 - 09

Harpley Chapel was closed and put up for sale in 1996. The years between 1984 and 1994 show some of the reasons for the decline of the Society. In 1983 there was a membership of twelve. In the decade that followed, eight people died and three moved away. There were no new members. In 1984 there were nine young people and one in 1990.

BLACKBOROUGH END

The Wesleyan Methodists earliest available records show ten members at 'Blackberry' End in 1837, reaching a total of 18 in 1843. Trustees were appointed in 1836 and the Chapel built in 1837. 'Pidgeon' was named as Society Steward in 1843. A Church Hall was built in 1875. A Worship Certificate was issued 17.3.1863, and a Marriage Certificate on 3.7.1900.

Membership 1885-1930

1885 - 14 1890 - 11	1895 - 41 1900 - 18	1905 - 09 1910 - 08	1915 - 10 1920 - 29	1925 - 23 1930 - 18

The Primitive Methodists. Mr Boldero was appointed assistant leader in 1880. Sunday School officials in 1881 were:- R Flood superintendent, John Sampson, secretary and R Berry, treasurer. The School was discontinued in 1887 *"in consequence of preaching house."*

Society Stewards from 1879:- R Berry, J Sampson, R Flood, H Able.

Society Stewards 1933-1990:- R.E Goodrum, S Pearce, F.W Alexander, G.R Humphryes, R Bartrum, E Pitcher,

Membership 1933-1990

1933 - 16 1940 - 11 1945 - 06	1950 - 07 1955 - 09 1960 - 13	1965 - 08 1970 - 08 1975 - 09	1980 - 06 1985 - 05 1990 - 04

The Chapel was closed in 1994 and is now a private dwelling.

Harpley notes:-
(1)Trustees appointed in 1898 were:- Robert Hammond, Edward Hammond and George Hammond (continuing trustees) and William Clarke gentleman, George W Haws labourer, William Rudd labourer, Thomas William Whitby labourer, Benjamin F Ward porter.
(2)Trustees appointed in 1911 were:- William Clarke, George William Haws, Thomas William Whitby, Benjamin Frederick Ward, (continuing) and Elisha Pilgrim labourer, Elizabeth Mountain married woman, Frederick Hammond platelayer, Harry Ramm shepherd, Jacob Hammond junr carter, John Gage Mountain wheelwright, Bessie Mountain spinster, Ethel Rose Hammond married woman, Charles Thomas Mountain blacksmith, Percy Edward Mountain carpenter, and James Mobbs labourer.

Chapter nineteen

WEST WINCH & EAST WINCH

WEST WINCH

The Wesleyan Methodists had a Society of 5 in 1837. Trustees were appointed on 1st June, 1861(1) and a Chapel built seating 120 people. Society Stewards in 1933 were C.H Elyard and Miss Cassell. After Methodist Union, the Chapel was called West Winch South and the PM Chapel West Winch North. In 1960, a trust was formed for both Chapels.

A new Sunday School was opened on 30th June 1964.

The Primitive Methodists had a Society of 3 in the first quarter of 1845 but fell to zero by the third. An account of Chapels and rooms in the Circuit, circa 1865, stated, *"we occupy a small place here the history of which may be had of Mr Offord of West Winch."*

The displeasure of the Circuit Committee was incurred in 1861 as is evident by the following minute, eg *"that in consequence of West Winch people being disposed to amalgamate with the New Connexion that on Good Friday we request Mr Lane to preach in this Chapel, or lecture on Judas etc."*

Brother C Whitehead became an accredited Local Preacher in 1864, and Philip George given liberty to speak in 1871. Efforts were made to obtain land for a new Chapel and sites included Cock Close, Ox Close and Bush Piece. On 25th March 1874, the Committee decided *"that a deputation be appointed to wait upon Mr Wake in connection with the purchasing of a piece of land in which to build a chapel."* It was decided that the Chapel would be *"19 wide and 30 feet long in the clear"*, have a boarded floor, a rostrum and a slated roof, *"that bord timber be laid in the walls 3 by 3½ to fasten the pew tops to"* and that the walls *"should be 14 inches except the south gable which shall be 9 inches."* Messrs Story & Bodger's tender for £176 was accepted. Arrangements for the foundation stone ceremony on Whit Monday were for Mr Lift to lay the stone and Rev. Howchin to preach the service.

The August meeting planned for the opening and fitting out of the Chapel, ie:- for steps to be placed at the entrance, for lamps to be fixed on the side walls, for 6 blinds, *"that Mr Seaman get the bills printed 100 and that the tea be ½ past 5 and price 1/-. That there be cocoa matting got for the isle of West Winch new chapel and mat for the door and carpet for platform."* E Daws was appointed treasurer. The Chapel was planned to open on 6th and 7th September 1874 with Rev. Howchin and Wm Lift preaching the opening services. Rev. Seaman was asked to let the sittings, *"and bring the money to the treasurer."* It was agreed *"that the price of sittings in West Winch chapel be ninepence each, unless one person shall hire as a whole pew, which shall be four shillings for the six sittings."*

Arrangements were made to bring the fittings of the old Chapel to Lynn, and for Rev. Seaman to *"appoint someone to clean the new chapel at West Winch on Friday evening next and that this meeting thinks Mrs Ringwood or Mrs George to be likely persons," and "that this meeting thinks £1.10.0 per year would be a fair thing for cleaning."*

John Alflatt of Sheffield made the gift of a clock. Brother Parnell was given liberty to speak in September 1875, and Brothers John Frost and James Gayten in December 1881. New trustees were appointed on 9th January 1900(2).

The Sunday School were allowed a library in 1878 and the trustees to buy land for a schoolroom in 1899. In 1897, C Hazel was secretary, followed by Miss George in 1899. In 1900 there were 14 teachers and 46 scholars, average attendance 35 - 6 over the age of 14.

Temperance. Band of Hope with 72 juvenile abstainers - 1900.

N&S Society Stewards from 1879:- T Offord, Jas Frost, T Reeder, C Hazle, W Slaughter, I Barrett, H Drew, W George, G Alcock, Miss Softley,

Mrs Coward, Mrs Crowe.

Membership West Winch North 1934-1940

1934-17	1935 - 17	1940 - 17

Membership West Winch South 1934 - 1950

1934-10	1935-12	1940-12	1945-19	1950-18

West Winch N & S 1956 - 1971

1956-20	1961-18	1965-16	1969-12	1971-09

EAST WINCH

The Wesleyan Methodists from 1900 to 1904 had two members. The Class was led by Narborough Society in 1902.

The Primitive Methodists had 17 people on trial in March 1838. During the next decade, numbers fluctuated from a high of 27 in 1841 to a low of 7 in 1847. Thomas Wright was the Class Leader in 1843. A Camp Meeting was planned in 1844 and Brother W Lane given liberty to speak in 1859. Mrs Hunter was asked in June 1863, *"to take the class at East Winch for the present."* Preaching took place in a cottage belonging to Mr Bunting. Books and four small forms were lent by the Circuit in 1865, *"to assist them in opening a Sabbath School."* The Preachers were asked in 1867 *"to make enquiry at East Winch as to the possibility or probability of obtaining land for a chapel."* A Circuit Meeting in 1869 decided *"that H Worth enquire when next at East Winch respecting the benches and testaments that were supplied from Lynn for the Sabbath School there, which has been discontinued for about 2 years."*

A Circuit meeting in 1908 decided *"that in view of the unsettled condition of the Society at East Winch, the following be appointed as deputation to visit the society and to endeavour to place things on a more satisfactory footing:- Rev. F.G Saville, Messrs Hunter, Rasberry, and G Alcock."* Efforts were made to obtain land, and in 1921 it was decided *"that The Rev R Holman, Mr W Hunter and Mr J Hunter be empowered to purchase a piece of land at East Winch and that the members of the meeting form the trust."*

The Chapel was built and dedicated in 1925/1926.

Sunday School commenced 1880. In 1900 there were 2 teachers and 23 scholars (average attendance 22). L Laws was secretary in 1897 and R Vincent in 1899. A report in 1915 stated *"East Winch discontinued during year."*

P.M Society Stewards from 1879:- W Downing, T Reed, A Goose, H Bonnett, W Hunter, Mrs Doughty, J Hunter, W Reed, H Teverson, S Seaman, A.T Storey, A Reynolds.

Membership 1934-1969

1934 - 21 1935 - 20	1940 - 15 1945 - 08	1950 - 07 1956 - 06	1961 - 05 1965 - 04	1969 - 03

The last service was held on 7th September 1969.

West Winch notes:-
(1)Wesleyan trustees appointed in 1861 were:- John Jackson, J Learmouth, Edward Holmes, Edward Eggett, Thomas Moore, Stephen Stott, Thomas Cressy.
(2)P.M trustees appointed in 1900 were:- Thomas F Offord and Philip L George, continuing, and William George, Charles Horle, Walter Slaughter, Thomas Daw, Isaac Barnett, John Watson, Richard Samuel Tipple, James Charles Frost.

Chapter twenty

EAST WALTON, GAYTON THORPE & WALPOLE CROSS KEYS

EAST WALTON

The Wesleyan Methodists have no available record of a presence.

The Primitive Methodists annual report to the Norwich District Meeting in 1877 (Lynn Station) stated, *"we have remissioned East Walton and formed a society of 4 members."* Land was leased from Mr Birbeck of Westacre and memorial stones for the Chapel were planned to be laid on Good Friday, 1889. The Chapel was dedicated on 30th June by Rev. R Church, and was opened on 7th July with Rev. G Shreeve, followed on 13th July by Rev. J Cooper. The cost was £200. It was designed for 100 sittings and 50 adherents. There was a tea meeting and lecture on 7th May 1894, for the new harmonium. Mr F Youngs was Chairman. A Chapel Committee was formed to work with the trustees in 1911(1). A Sunday School Convention was planned on 21st May 1921.

Sunday School started in 1890. In 1900 there were 4 teachers and 14 scholars (average attendance 10 - 3 were over 14 years old). Miss A Loades - secretary in 1897- Mr J Lords in 1899.

Temperance. There was a Band of Hope - no numbers given.

Society Stewards from 1879 included:- J Jude, Mr Bilham, C Back, J Edwards, E Jackson, W Jackson, A Rowe, C Keeley, S Wilson, B Wilson.

Membership from 1913

1913 - 16	1925 - 11	1940 - 10	1956 - 04	1969 - 03
1915 - 13	1929 - 08	1945 - 10	1961 - 04	
1920 - 11	1935 - 08	1950 - 07	1965 - 01	

GAYTON THORPE

The Wesleyan Methodists have no records available of a presence in the village.

The Primitive Methodists had a Society of 11 in December 1836. By 1848 this had risen to 16. In between, numbers fluctuated from a high of 33 in 1844 to a low of 6 in 1839. Brothers B Sussens and L Knoll were given liberty to speak in June 1863. Preaching was undertaken in two cottages, *"principally at Mr Sussum's."*

An offer by Mr Henry Birbeck of West Acre to lease a piece of land for the erection of a Chapel, for the annual rental of 5/-, was accepted by the Circuit Committee. Trustees were appointed on 2nd December 1901(1), and a deed was signed on 1st April, 1902. The lease was valid for 50 years and renewable for a further 50. The Circuit Meeting of March 1902, approved *"the sketch of plans for Gayton Thorpe chapel not to cost only a little over £100."* The Chapel was consecrated in 1902 at a total cost of £180. It had seats for 90. There is no record of a Sunday School .

Society Stewards from 1879 included:- G Allcock, J.C Rye, Mr Bray, Mr Goodbody, Mrs M Bray, H.W Bray.

Membership 1913- 1969

1913 - 13 1915 - 12 1920 - 06	1925 - 07 1929 - 06 1934 - 09	1940 - 10 1945 - 11 1950 - 05	1954 - 05 1961 - 06 1969 - 05

WALPOLE CROSS KEYS

Walpole Cross Keys joined the Lynn Circuit from the Wisbech Circuit in 1935. It had been registered as a place of Religious Worship on 13th March 1885. The records of certification were cancelled on 1st December 1978(1).

Trusts were appointed in 1902(2) and 1952(3).

Society Stewards 1935-1969

H.J Jewson, Miss L Rudderham, W.R James, W Pack, J.R Hannah, G Goodwin, Rev. G.L Hodson.

Membership 1936-1969

1936 - 08 1940 - 05 1945 - 08	1950 - 21 1956 - 25 1961 - 25	1965 - 17 1968 - 04 1969 - 04

East Walton notes:-
(1)The 1911 Chapel Committee were:- Messrs W Jackson, J Loades, W Elmer, W Ketteringham, E Loades and Miss Loades.

Gayton Thorpe notes:-
(1)Trustees appointed in 1901 were:- James Rasberry, Francis Franklin, George Allcock, Robert Nelson, Edmund Davey, George W Shinn, William Savage, James Henry Martin and Anthony Proctor.

Walpole Cross Keys notes:-
(1)Source:- Lynn News & Advertiser 5.1.1979.
(2)Members of the 1902 trust were:- William Simpson, William Londen, Henry Emmerson, James Robinson, Edward Pitcher, William H Flint, Robert Large, Jas. Smith, Geo A Miller, Walter Jackson, Luke Simpson, Jas. Simpson, John Carter.
(3)Members of the 1952 trust were:- George Venni, Lewis Barnes, George A Goodwin, Sophia A Goodwin, Linda M Rudderham, Eveline Hillard, Miss Gladys Rowe, Bertha E Smith, Sarah Ann Sadler, Wilfred Russell James, William Delamore, Miriam A Reeve, Vera Clarke, Henry Emmerson, Eleanor Margaret Jewson, Wilfred Hills.

Chapter twenty-one

TILNEY ALL SAINTS & SADDLEBOW

TILNEY ALL SAINTS

The Wesleyan Methodists had a Society of 11 people in 1837. From this nucleus developed a strong Society, as follows:-

1838 11	1839 11	1840 14	1841 32	1842 30	1843 29

Mr Johnson was the Society Steward in 1838. John Johnson was named in 1840 and J Johnson in 1843.

A Wesleyan Minister, the Reverend J.B Holroyd, agreed to the purchase of a Chapel and land from William Alexander and on 14th and 15th January 1831, the property was conveyed to him by appointment and release. The Chapel could seat 150 people.

Sunday School. In 1886, there were 56 Scholars in eight classes and a Sunday School Committee of ten people(1). The Anniversary was held on the first Sunday in May, at 10.30, 2.30 and 6.15pm. The minute book records that *"on the following Monday children and teachers meet at the Chapel at 10 o'clock parade the village starting at 10.30 punctually. All officers not there at the time stated except in very urgent cases to be fined 2/-. Luncheon for the children at 12 o'clock. Bro L Robinson to provide six tea makers and to ask Mrs Alexander to help Mrs Warwick cut bread and butter."* (This was for a public tea meeting at 3.pm). *"Bro G Robinson to ask Mr W Failes for the use of his field for the children to play in. After tea a public meeting at 7 o'clock. Bro Robinson undertakes to get all the provisions for lunch and tea also ½ peck of sweets for children."*

The children were given a tea on 22nd December and fifty oranges and half a peck of nuts were given to them.

Methodist fête c.1930(3) (Acknowledgements Messrs Jewsons of Lynn)

In 1888, James Mawby was school secretary, followed by R Garrett in 1890. At this time the teachers were:- Joseph Smith, Robert Garrett, Charles Parnell, Eleanor Johnson, Eda Robinson and Eliza Smith.

An Anniversary was held on Sunday 7th May 1939. Pastor J.V Staton conducted services at 2.25 and 6.15pm. On the Monday, scholars were given a tea at 4pm. It was followed by a public meeting at 7pm; the chairman was Mr Bugg of Harpley. An address was given by the Rev. H.G Rolls.

The last service was held on 29th December 1968.

Society Stewards from 1933:- J Reeve, H Jermey, N Robinson, Dr R Reeve, A Pepper, A Bland.

Membership 1933-1968

1933 - 19 1935 - 14 1940 - 19	1945 - 27 1950 - 21 1956 - 28	1961 - 22 1965 - 24 1968 - 14

SADDLEBOW

The Primitive Methodists. No information available.

The Wesleyan Methodists had a Society and built a Chapel. Included in the trustees appointed on 25th March 1886, were local residents:- G.W Scott, a market gardener, and Robert Chenery, George Offord and William Spratt, who were labourers. Trustees were appointed in 1921, 1949(1)and 1962.

Membership 1886-1960

1886 - 11 1890 - 06 1896 - 06 1900 - 07	1905 - 14 1910 - 09 1916 - 07 1920 - 03	1925 - 06 1930 - 06 1936 - 06 1940 - 05	1945 - 02 1950 - 04 1955 - 06 1960 - 03

Society Stewards 1933 - 1960 included:- Mr Raynor, E.W Dodman, A.J Powers, R.H Lewis, G Venni, T Gray.

Saddlebow came off the plan in 1962. Tribute was paid to Mr and Mrs Gray and Mrs Gorbould the organist, who, for several years, had borne the responsibility of keeping the Chapel open.

The last service was held on 7th April 1962.

Tilney All Saints notes:-

(1)The Sunday School Committee comprised:- Valentine Nelson superintendent, Leonard Robinson assistant superintendent, George Robinson treasurer, Joseph Smith secretary, Charles Claxton, Joseph Mawby, Emma Warwick, George Norton, James Mawby and Thomas Warwick.

(2)The public tea for which tickets were 6d, consisted of the following main ingredients:-$3\frac{1}{2}$ stone bread, 3 stone cake half plain half plum, $3\frac{1}{2}$ lbs cheese, 8lbs butter, $1\frac{1}{4}$lbs tea, 10lbs sugar, $\frac{1}{2}$ peck shrimps, $\frac{1}{2}$cwt coals for heating water.

(3)Bean bag thrower - Lord Fermoy. Boy in white flannels, school blazer and cap - Norman Robinson.

Saddlebow notes:-

(1)Trustees appointed on 2.4.1949 were:- George Coe Saddlebow, Ernest Sketcher King's Lynn, Horace Burman King's Lynn, William Joseph Panton King's Lynn, Reginald Hubert Lewis St.Mary's, John William Calton Islington, Leonard W.A Barrett Gaywood, Algernon Caley St.Germans, Edward James Gaskins Islington, Cecil James Mallett King's Lynn, Mrs Ethel Mary Calton Islington, Arthur William Freeman King's Lynn, Mrs Florence Elizabeth Lewis St.Mary's, Thomas Arthur Gray Saddlebow, Mrs Violet Grace Green King's Lynn, Miss Kenya Elizabeth Carter King's Lynn, Miss Fernley Marjorie Oliver King's Lynn, Edmund Brown and John Ward Terrington St.Clement.

Chapter twenty-two

LONDON ROAD (SOUTH)

The Wesleyan Methodists built a Chapel in 1888, which could seat 350 (see chapter 2). A trust was established 1st December 1883(1).

Dates from the Records

28th October 1931. A Scenic Bazaar held in the schoolroom. Admission:- 6d, children 4d. It was opened by Ivan J Thatcher, Esq, with the objective of raising £100 for the London Road trust fund. Chairman was William Thompson.

23rd May 1935. Jubilee Celebrations were held. A special visitor was the President of the Methodist Conference, the Rev. W Younger, who preached at 4pm. There was a public tea at 5.30 followed by a public meeting at 7pm.

Jubilee ticket 1935

22nd/23rd February 1939. A Bazaar entitled 'A Trip to the Low Countries' was held in the schoolroom.

In November 1961, a District Sub-Committee, having considered the close proximity of the two Methodist Churches in London Road, had agreed to a new Church being built on the St. James site and that the St. James and London Road South Societies should unite and worship at St. James in the meantime.

Rev. Harry Lockwood took over pastoral responsibility for both Churches in 1963.

Society Stewards 1933-1964

O.L Troman, W.S Harris, C.K Butt, R Harris,
H Plympton, E Burton, G Rix, R Chapman, L Finbow,
Miss A Bocking, J.R Mindham, G.W Ward, E.H Garfoot.

Membership 1933-1964

1933 - 58 1935 - 77	1940 - 88 1945 - 120	1950 - 109 1956 - 100	1961 - 83 1964 - 75

The last services were held on 30th August 1964, with a special service at 8pm.

Notes:-
(1)The1883 trustees were:- J Jackson factor, W Thompson the elder timber merchant, W.L. Armes factor, Alfred Jermyn draper, J Paul shipowner, R Whiteman baker, Edward Eggett coal merchant, J.A. Hillam stone mason, W Wildbur, W.R. Smith, Robert Bush baker, Charles Allen, F.A. Curson, B Curson hatter, F Ollett, R Thompson, W Thompson the younger.

Chapter twenty-three

WEST NEWTON, FAIR GREEN & PENTNEY

WEST NEWTON

The Wesleyan Methodists earliest available record show a Society present in 1843. King Edward VII gave facilities for preaching between 1902 and 1910(1).

The Primitive Methodists had met *"at cottages"* since 1823. In 1837 there were 21 members plus 9 on trial. Class Leader was Ann Neale. There was a highpoint of 43 in 1842 and a low of 18 in 1837, In 1848 there were 25 members. Preachers used the cottage of Mrs Kelk, a widow. Around 1860, the Society moved to Mr Piggin's cottage.

On 25th November 1864, a Memorial was written to HRH the Prince of Wales requesting permission for a site for a Chapel. The reply from Sandringham was *"I am desired to express the regret of HRH the Prince of Wales that he does not feel himself at liberty to comply with your request."*

In the Spring of 1870 open-air services were planned. In June 1872, the Circuit Authorities agreed *"that if any person at West Newton will give us accommodation or be willing to open their house for religious services, we are quite willing to appoint them preaching."* Three months later the Committee decided *"that the next travelling preacher who goes to Wolverton shall accompany Bro Claxton to West Newton to see what can be done for the better meeting of the class and make enquiry after a house in which to preach."*

The Circuit Meeting in 1874 agreed *"that we offer the stand formerly used as a preacher's desk at West Winch to the West Newton Society for five shillings, painted."*

On 30th November 1904, the Circuit Authorities recorded appreciation to Mr and Mrs Dye of West Newton, for their services.

A Deed of 18th March 1907, registered an agreement between HM the King and the Primitive Methodists for the use of a rented room as a preaching place.

Society Stewards 1879-1958:- T Kelk, J Gent, H Dye, G Painter, W Fenn, Mrs Smith, G Hunt, F Dack, Mrs Dack.

The last service was held on 6th April 1958.

FAIR GREEN

The Wesleyan Methodists had a Society at Tower End and a Chapel at Middleton but no presence at Fairgreen.

The Primitive Methodists earliest records show a Society in 1844. Numbers varied quarterly from a high of 12 to 1. James Eggleton was assistant leader in 1845. The Society was allowed to hire a preaching house for worship in 1866. A Sunday School started in 1881 but was discontinued in 1884 as *"the three teachers have left the place having no one to carry it on."* Brother Sampson was put on the plan as an approved Local Preacher in 1882 and a cottage was hired for twelve months at a rent of £3 per annum in 1899. Also in 1899, a committee of management was formed(1).

Mr J.C Frost was accorded a vote of thanks *"for the great interest and arduous labour he has put into the cause at Fair Green(2)."* The purchase of land for £15, owned by the Shepherd's Club, was sanctioned on 9th April 1902, on the condition the vendors paid their own legal expenses. This was not agreed by the vendors for on 10th May, the Committee agreed *"that we give our sanction for the purchase of land at Fair Green on the vendor's conditions though we consider these unusual and unbusinesslike."* (The vendors had insisted that the Circuit Authorities paid the legal fees). The Society received permission to build a Chapel in September 1902. The new Chapel opened on 9th September 1903.

The Chapel cost £200 and had 64 sittings and 50 adherents. A Letter of appreciation was sent to the Society on 1st March 1915, *"for their enterprise in commencing a Sunday School."*

Society Stewards from 1879: J Berry, J.C Frost, M Barrett, A Arnold, W.C Bailey, H Riches, E.J Culpin, Mr Haverson, E Cornwall, Mrs E Gould, J Watts, Mrs Boddy, W Sutton, A Seaman.

Membership from 1913

1913 - 13	1920 - 11	1929 - 13	1940 - 03	1950 - 06
1915 - 15	1925 - 08	1935 - 18	1945 - 04	1955 - 03

The last service was held on 27th November 1955.

PENTNEY

The Primitive Methodists. No available record.

The Wesleyan Methodists had a 150 seat Chapel. Trustees appointed in 1882, were James Ellis of Pentney and W Arnold of Narborough, a shoemaker. Local trustees appointed in 1919 were:- William H Scase, George Gutteridge and Charles Rasberry.

A trustees minute dated 29th January 1924, records, *"the treasurer was asked to write to the caretaker asking that the goat be removed from the shed and stable."*

Society Stewards 1933-1951: Mrs Skipper, W Elsegood.

Membership 1885-1951

1885 - 21	1900 - 13	1915 - 08	1930 - 13	1945 - 04
1890 - 18	1905 - 10	1920 - 16	1935 - 08	1950 - 03
1895 - 23	1910 - 08	1925 - 11	1940 - 05	1951 - 03

The last service was held on 28th November 1951.

West Newton notes:-
(1)Experiences of an East Anglian Methodist: Alderman Alfred Jermyn J.P. JROLM MACP3 Vol 8L 1913.

Fair Green notes:-
(1)The management committee were:- A.J Wardle, W Savage, G Hammond, J.C Frost, J Watson, J Kidd and R Tipple.
(2)Mr J.C Frost was a Local Preacher who lived in Melbourne Street, King's Lynn. He was known as the "Bishop of Fair Green" and walked from Lynn on most Sundays to support Fair Green Society. He was a trustee, treasurer, and advanced money to the Society free of interest.

Chapter twenty-four

MASSINGHAM

The Wesleyan Methodists were present from the Swaffham Circuit and had a 155 seat Chapel.

The Primitive Methodists had a Society that varied in membership between 14 and 49 in the period 1837 to 1848. The leader was George Sculpher a Local Preacher. Preaching took place in a Chapel hired from Mr Jarvis of King's Lynn. In 1838, Messrs William Claxton, Everitt and Roye, were asked *"to take out and take charge of the furniture in Great Massingham Chapel belonging to the Connexion."* The next Quarterly Meeting asked the trustees to try and continue the school.

In 1867 the Circuit Committee decided *"that we accept the offer of land measured by Mr Grummitt 11yds x 9yds for £30 for a new chapel at Massingham and that we apply to the District Building Committee for sanction."*

In 1869, the Circuit Authorities were trying for a valid title for land they had agreed to purchase. A year later, legalities settled, subscriptions for the Chapel were solicited. They were also allowed to pull down stone walls and clean bricks on the purchased land to show that they had taken possession. Meanwhile the Revs. Rous and Howchin, were asked to write to builders they thought fit for tenders. One of £147 from Mr W Curtis was accepted. A memorial stone was laid on 5th August 1870 by Mr W Lift. Problems in obtaining matching bricks resulted in the builder being told that the Committee did not mind *"if the colour of the brick do not match for the back wall and rather than the work should be delayed we agree to allow 2/6d for every 1000 fetched from Barney providing the Chapel be ready for opening by the last week in September or the first Sunday in October."* The Circuit Committee felt that if the windows were as large as at Shouldham *"they are sufficient and proportionate enough."*

It was agreed that illumination would be provided by four lamps, two on each side. The Revs. Rous and Howchin were asked to obtain suitable ones. Begging cards were printed for Massingham and Gayton.

The Chapel opened on 9th October 1870. Sermons were preached by Revs. W Sparling and R Howchin. It had sittings for 150 and 50 adherents. Brother N Claxton was appointed treasurer, and Brothers E Dawson and W Everard, seat stewards.

The fittings of the old Chapel were taken to Lynn for sale; the proceeds of which were added to Chapel funds.

In 1871, H Nobbs was given permission to speak and the Society was allowed to have a few stones from the old stable block in County Court Road, Lynn, for a fence. The trustees were rebuked for allowing a meeting of the Agricultural Union in the Chapel contrary to the rules of the Connexion, and told that if any person should hold a similar meeting *"that decisive steps will be taken with such persons."*

In 1881, trustees were allowed to improve the floor in the Chapel, *"either by raising it or by digging away the soil, and that they have a service in connection with it to help to pay for it."*

New trustees were appointed on 3rd June 1901(1). In 1904, the trustees were given permission for a tablet in the Chapel in memory of Mrs Moore. A Centenary Camp Meeting was planned for June 1910 and a Sunday School convention in 1912, *"before harvest commences."* A Rally was planned in 1914.

Sunday School. In 1865 there were 6 teachers and 22 scholars. In 1870, Massingham was not listed, but later that year received permission *"to raise a Sabbath School."* W Everard was appointed superintendent, E Dawson assistant superintendent and secretary and Brother Roye treasurer. A Sunday School was re-established in 1871 with 7 teachers and 24 scholars. This closed, but re-opened in 1875 with H Roye superintendent, N Coe vice superintendent and treasurer and J Daws secretary. This did not last long, for in 1882, the Committee decided *"that steps be taken with the friends of Massingham to induce them to form a Sunday School."* In 1897, the secretary was F Goll and in 1899, Miss Roye. There were 6 teachers and 47 scholars in 1900 with average attendance of 35, with 3 of the scholars were over 14 years.

Temperance. There were 40 juvenile abstainers and 5 adult abstainers.

Society Stewards from 1879:- W Claxton, N Coe, T Moore, J Hubbard, F Whitby, J Caller, A Coker, Mrs Moore.

Membership from 1913-1950

1913 - 16 1915 - 10	1920 - 13 1925 - 11	1929 - 06 1933 - 11	1935 - 13 1940 - 14	1945 - 10 1950 - 09

The Society were transferred to the Swaffham Circuit.

Notes:-
(1)Trustees appointed in 1901 were:- Henry Roye, continuing, and John Daws, Joshua Seaman, George Goll, Fred Goll, Thomas Moore, Herbert Boldero, Robert King.

Chapter twenty-five

WATLINGTON

The Wesleyan Methodists had a membership from 1837-1843, as follows:-

1837 09	1838 10	1839 09	1840 14	1841 19	1842 14	1843 11

There was also a Chapel with ten trustees(1). The Society Steward from 1838-1843 was Mr Allen. Trustees were appointed on 12th May 1860(2). The Chapel could accommodate 115 people. Mr J Jackson was Society Steward in 1918 and Mrs Chapman and Miss Crosby shared the role in 1930.

Class Leaders 1885-1944

W Spratt, Wm Garrett, Mr Dawson, J Jackson, The Minister, J.H Dew, Mrs J Chapman, Mrs Woodhouse.

Membership 1885-1944

1885 - 17 1890 - 09 1894 - 16 1895 - 11	1900 - 10 1905 - 06 1910 - 05 1917 - 06	1920 - 10 1925 - 18 1930 - 13 1936 - 06	1940 - 09 1944 - 05

The last service was held on 2nd April 1944.

The Primitive Methodists earliest available records show a Society of 12 in 1843. This peaked at 25 in September 1844, and fell back to 13 in 1846 prompting the Circuit Authorities to plan a Missionary Meeting *"as early as possible next quarter."* In 1851 it was planned *"that Watlington be missioned $^1/_2$10 & $^1/_2$2 by two preachers."* The Circuit minutes hint of a Chapel in January 1859, i.e. *"that we accept the mortgage deed of Watlington estate if it doth* *not enlarge the expences."* In August, the Committee felt it could not sanction £50 to be given to build the new Chapel, however, Mr Howchin (the Superintendent Minister) was advised *"to make the best bargain he can and report it to another meeting."* Later, the District Building Committee gave permission to build the new Chapel, and arrangements were made for the Chapel foundation stone to be laid on Wednesday 21st September, with a tea meeting afterwards.

The Chapel was built in 1859 at a cost of £84.3.6 (£31.13.6 was raised and £50 borrowed at 5% interest). There was seating for 60 in pews and 30 in free seats. It was opened for Divine Service on 30th October 1859. A piece of spare land measuring 12 feet x 30 feet adjoined the Chapel.

The Society were given a minor rebuke by the Circuit Committee in 1862, as follows:- *"that, the Watlington friends be advised the committee are very sorry they were so disappointed on Sunday last, and hope the local brethren will be more punctual in future."* However, in 1865 they were given permission *"to improve the interior of their Chapel."*

The trustees were recommended to pay back £30 that had been called in, plus interest, in 1867 and borrow £30 from Mrs Forster of Harpley. The Reverend R Howchin was asked in the same year, *"to see to the state of the building of the Chapel at Watlington which is said to be falling."* The trustees were given permission *"to put up an iron pallisade in front of their Chapel"* in 1879, and three years later *"to repair the windows and door, also to build a water closet and copper house when they have the means."*

In 1900, the Chapel had an income of £8.10.4 of which pew rents accounted for £1.10.11 and rent for the Sunday School 10/-. Watlington, with several other P.M Societies in the southern half of the Lynn Circuit, was transferred into the newly formed Fincham Branch in 1904. (It became a separate Circuit in 1912).

Society Stewards 1879-1900

T Bowden junr, W Warren, J Smith.

Sunday Schools

1865 - 6 teachers and 43 scholars
1871 - 5 teachers and 45 scholars
1900 - 4 teachers and 24* scholars
*10 aged over 14 years - average attendance 18.

A report dated 31st December, 1883 stated *"Watlington School discontinued because no teacher to attend to it but hope to recommence it soon."*

J Smith was the Sunday School secretary in 1897 a role filled by G Smith in 1899.

Temperance. There was a juvenile Band of Hope in 1900.

Notes:-
(1)Wesleyan trustees named were:- Mrs Allen, Henry Leverington, Thos Green, Thos Martin, Chas Bootman, J Batterbee, Edw Colman, Wm Colman, Thos Peeps, Lionel Langford.
(2)Wesleyan trustees appointed in 1860 were:- John Jackson, George Cawthorne, George Scott, Thomas Leman, Edward Eggett, James Jennings, James Learmouth, Edward Holmes, William Henry Boyce, T Hudson, M Failes, Michael Starling and Thomas Porter.

Chapter twenty-six

TOWER STREET

The Wesleyan Methodists opened this imposing building in 1813 (see chapter 2). New trustees appointed in 1874(1).

Some Class Leaders prior to 1882 included:- Mr Gridley, William Laird, John Kenny, W Wildbur, J.A Hillam, George Cooper, Mrs M Keeble, Dr W Dale M.D., John Jackson, Mrs M.A Jackson, A Scott, W Whiteman, J Paul, E Eggett, Alfred Jermyn, J Register, Mrs Wise, Mrs J Burch, Mrs W Jackson, Mrs M Kendrick, Mrs Wildbur, Mrs Ranshaw, Mrs E.A Laird.

Sir Alfred Jermyn

Some long-serving members in 1882 included:- Susan Eggett (1821), John Ashby (1830), Amy Regester (1830), Elizabeth Millington (1833), Mathew Creak (1836), Elizabeth Mallett (1836), Robert Whiteman (1836), Hannah Plowright (1837), Susan Reed (1838) and Robert Rands (1840).

Special Events included Centenary Celebrations in 1913, during which the Chapel was renovated and electric lighting installed. Regular scenic Bazaars were held for fund raising, these included:- 'All in a Garden' Bazaar on 16/17th February 1932. Opened by Lord Fermoy MP on 16th, and J Harwood Catleugh Esq. on 17th, and a 'Dutch' Bazaar on 18th/19th February 1936, which was opened by Mrs Somerset A. Maxwell on the 18th and Mrs P.T Chatterton on the 19th.

Minutes from the Leaders' Meeting

1st October 1920. *"With regard to the noise caused by children in the galleries on the Sunday evening, it was agreed that some arrangement should be made to get them sandwiched between grown-ups downstairs."*

2nd June 1921. Memorial to the Fallen. This was fully discussed and it was decided to erect a tablet in stone or marble; a number of people were elected from Tower Street, London Road and North End to see it carried out. Mr C.H Lemmon, treasurer, Mr J.M Barrett, secretary.

25th August 1921. Rev. C.A Green referred to the loss sustained by the Church at Tower Street by the death of Sir Alfred Jermyn. Mr Norman was appointed leader of the late Sir A Jermyn's class.

22nd February 1924. Sir Alfred Jermyn's Bequest mentioned: Ten deserving members shared £4.10.0.

16th February 1933. Distribution of Smith's Charity decided. Thirty people received 2 cwt coal each plus money (3 tons coal from Oakes @ 36/- per ton £5.8.0. Total coal + cash £15.6.0).

Society Stewards 1933-1943 included:- E Flowerday, H.E Munns, J.S Piling, L.W.A Barrett, C Eyles, H Verry, C Young.

Membership 1933-1943

1933 - 182 1935 - 157	1940 - 159 1941 - 142	1942 - 180 1943 - 187

The Chapel had final services on Sunday 5th August 1943 and was taken off the plan. People continued to meet in the Chapel (54 in 1944) but numbers gradually declined (12 in 1945).

Notes:-
(1)Trustees appointed on 26th August 1874, were:- Jonathan Jackson, Benjamin Laird, Robert Faux, William Laird, George Scott, Alex Ormiston, George Crook, William Thompson, Thos Ashby Jackson, William Linay Armes, Alfred Jermyn, Robert Wise, Robert Whiteman, J Richardson Cossens, J Paul, Edward Eggett, Robert Bush, Thos Verry, James Regester.

Chapter twenty-seven

ROUGHAM

The Wesleyan Methodists. No available records.

The Primitive Methodists had 34 members in 1837. In 1838, Mary Ann Manning was Leader of a female class of 15 and Henry Frost Leader of a male class of 20 (both were Local Preachers). In 1863, a hired Chapel was used, with affairs managed by Edward Manning. A Circuit Meeting of May 1877 decided *"that if the matter of detail can be arranged Mr Lift, the architect and Mr Curtis of Litcham, the tender of the latter gentleman for building Rougham Chapel for £270 after allowing £54.10. for old materials be accepted. Gross tender £324.10. - Nett £270.0."* A Chapel was built in 1877 by Mr Curtis. It had 210 sittings and 50 adherents.

Sunday School. In 1846, 8 teachers and 50 scholars; 1865, 19 teachers and 108 scholars; 1871, 23 teachers and 129 scholars; 1900, 8 teachers and 40 scholars. In 1898 G Howell was secretary followed by W Bunfield in 1899.

Temperance. A Band of Hope with 51 juvenile abstainers.

Society Stewards 1879-1932 included:- J.T Sculpher, E Hewing, S Osborne, W Hooks, A Durrant.

Membership 1913-1932

1913 - 18 1915 - 15	1920 - 13 1923 - 13	1925 - 12 1932 - 25

Rougham Society were transferred to the Swaffham Circuit in 1933 following discussions that began in 1901.

Chapter twenty-eight

THE FINCHAM BRANCH

In 1901, the P.M. Societies on the Fincham side were consulted as to whether they were willing to form a Branch of the Lynn Circuit. In 1904, the Fincham Branch was formed. It comprised Fincham, Marham, Wereham, Shouldham Thorpe, Shouldham, Magdalen, Runcton Holme, Tottenhill, Watlington and Wormegay. In a special resolution at the Fincham Branch Quarterly Meeting, held at Wereham on 29th May 1912, Fincham became a separate Circuit. Later Fincham Circuit amalgamated with the Downham Market Circuit.

FINCHAM

The Wesleyan Methodists had a Society present with a 160 seat Chapel in the Downham Market Circuit.

The Primitive Methodists had a Society which varied between 78 and 62 members. A Chapel was built in 1835 with a seating capacity of 200 (120 in pews and 80 free sittings). The Chapel was enlarged in 1858 by adding 12 feet to the length. At the same time, a new gallery across one end was installed, with four new windows and new pews below.

Trustees c.1860 were:- Thomas Bywater, Everard Pank and Richard Steele. A piece of land was given by William Bywater in 1863 for a schoolroom. This was designed to be opened as a day school and this trust amalgamated with the Chapel trust by mutual consent.

Sunday School. In 1846 there were 5 teachers and 28 scholars, which rose to 11 teachers and 67 scholars in 1865. In 1871 there were 10 teachers and 60 scholars and in 1900, 6 teachers and 43 scholars. The secretary in 1898 was C Woods.

A Connexional day school opened in 1870 with 1 Teacher and 30 Scholars. Receipts for the year were £8.0.9½ and expenditure £5.6.0. The numbers of scholars increased to 40 in 1875.

The school was supported by the weekly fees of the children (pence), an annual tea, public meeting and by private subscriptions. In 1864, the Circuit recommended the trust to engage Miss Crisp, a teacher, at a salary of £5 per year and the *"childrens' pence."* The trustees did not follow up this suggestion and the Circuit Committee had to write to Miss Crisp with their apologies.

A New Chapel foundation stone was laid on 22nd April 1878 by William Lift, who arranged payment for the builder. (The money was paid before the Chapel was opened). It had palisading and a boundary wall included in the price. Seats were let at 9d each. The building was insured for £200. A new school was planned in 1901 and built in 1903. The Chapel was altered in 1904.

Society Stewards 1879-1900: Mr Simmons, Mr Taylor, Mr Hammond, F Barker.

MARHAM

The Wesleyan Methodists had a 130 seat Chapel in the Downham Market Circuit.

The Primitive Methodists had a Society that varied between 20 and 48 in the period 1837-1848. They met in a Chapel leased by James Raven for the term of 50 years at a rent of £6 per annum. (Mr Raven died in January 1838). Trustees were:- Francis Burton, John Hewing and Thomas Ketteringham. A dispute occurred in 1872, between the Circuit Quarterday Board and Mr B...of Marham, who refused to pay rent of 10/- per year for the Sunday School, to the Chapel trustees. Mr Nurse (a solicitor used by the Circuit) was asked to write a letter to the parties, *"who have locked the chapel against the connexion authorities in the Marham society."*

As a result E Hewing was appointed superintendent, Robert Harris, secretary and assistant superintendent and George Neville, treasurer. Mr B.. was requested to give up the key of the schoolbox, and the balance held belonging to the School, *"without any further unpleasantness."* The Marham authorities had been allowed to borrow Lynn School flags and banners for their anniversary and to buy wood to complete the platform. The Reverend H Gunns was asked to write to Brother B... of Marham *"requesting him to give up the platform, flags, etc. belonging to the school, into the hands of Bro Edward Hewing at once, as we do not wish to resort to any stringent measures."*

Land was purchased from Mr J Able for £20 in 1878 and a trust formed(1). A new Chapel, measuring 42x24 feet, was built in 1879 by Mr Butter for £519. It was intended to be opened on 21st and 22nd September, but was deferred to 28th September on account of the late harvest.

Society Steward 1879-1900:- E Hewing.

Sunday School comprised 5 teachers and 30 scholars in 1846, 14 teachers and 90 scholars in 1865 and in 1871, 10 teachers and 85 scholars. In 1900 there were 10 teachers and 57 scholars.

WEREHAM

The Wesleyan Methodists had a Chapel with 120 seats.

The Primitive Methodists met in a room belonging to Mr Pilgrim. He built a Chapel in 1871 and fitted it out, for an annual rent of £4. Brothers John and Charles Pilgrim were the seat stewards and Brother Barker the treasurer. John Pilgrim was also the Sunday School superintendent. Land was purchased in 1893 and trustees appointed(1). An iron Chapel was built in 1898 at a cost of £160.

Society Stewards 1879-1900:- H Firman, H Head, F Lambert, J Lavender, S. J Dane.

Sunday School began in 1870. In 1871 there were 5 teachers and 27 children. It closed in 1877 because the Chapel had been given up.

SHOULDHAM THORPE

The Primitive Methodists. Membership varied from 8 to 27 from 1837-1848. A Chapel was built in 1849, copyhold, for £107.15.3. John Ogden was treasurer. There was seating for 106 people, 82 in pews and 24 free seats. In 1849 there were 54 members.

Sunday School. In 1865 there were 6 teachers and 74 scholars. Records do not show a school in 1871, but a new school started in 1875 with 4 teachers and 24 scholars. Another Sunday School in the village was called the "Methodist Free Church Sunday School" and one local member was rebuked for aiding this school. Secretary in 1898 was C Wilson and in 1899, Mr Harris.

Temperance. There were 5 adult total abstainers.

SHOULDHAM

The Wesleyan Methodists had a Society and a 200 seat Chapel in the Downham Market Circuit.

The Primitive Methodists. Between 1842 and 1848, membership varied between 15 and 29. Services were held in Mr Box's cottage. In 1846, a Chapel was leased for 14 years from Mr Charles Howy. (The trustees were Charles Pleasance, William Rust and William Adams). With a view to a new Chapel, Mr Proctor was authorised to buy a property in 1865, at a reserve bid of £100, or appoint someone *"whom he thinks most proper to do so."* The Circuit Committee agreed in December 1865, *"that the plans and specification for Shouldham Chapel be received except the stained glass and that the carriage for the materials be done by the trustees and friends."* The Chapel was built in 1866.

Sunday School was established in 1875. Mr A Proctor superintendent, Mr Bowe vice, Jabez Collison secretary and F Pikett treasurer. The Chapel was enlarged for the needs of the Sunday School in 1877, and a new school planned in 1893. W Stockdale was secretary in 1898. In 1900 there were 6 teachers and 48 children.

Society Stewards 1879-1900 included:- E Watts, R Green, F Grief.

A meeting of the Circuit Authorities in March 1894, called the attention of the trustees *"to the extraordinary amount of money spent on coal during the last year and desires them to take immediate steps in the matter."*

WIGGENHALL ST MARY MAGDALEN

The Wesleyan Methodists had a Society of 14 people in 1837, this increased to 21 in 1843. Mrs Starr was Society Steward in 1840, followed by T Green in 1843. The Chapel had seats for 150.

The Primitive Methodists had a society of 29 in 1845. Brother Woffen was the Society Steward in 1847. A Chapel was purchased in 1854 for £56.3.4 with sittings for 110 people (74 in pews and 36 free seats). However, it became so dilapidated that it was pulled down in 1862 and a new Chapel built for £295.

Society Stewards 1879-1900 included:- J Taylor, H Able, J Robertson, J Whistle, T Whistle, G Carter, H Fox, W Barber.

Sunday School. In 1865 there were 10 teachers and 68 scholars. In 1871 - 12 teachers and 90 scholars, and in 1900 - 16 teachers and 89 scholars.

Temperance. There were 36 juvenile and 9 adult abstainers.

RUNCTON HOLME

The Primitive Methodists had a Society of 17 members in 1844, which rose to 23, fell back to 7 and temporarily faded away in 1847. Services were held in a small Chapel belonging to Mr Gutteridge in 1860. Mr Brooks was appointed leader of the Society in 1864. In 1876, a piece of land 28 x 21 feet, that included the Chapel was bought from Mr Gutteridge for £42. A Chapel was built in 1881 for a sum stated by the Circuit Committee *"that was not to exceed £100."* Trustees were appointed(1).

Society Steward 1879-1900. H Webb.

New Trustees were appointed in 1898.

Sunday School started in 1875 but was discontinued in 1887.

TOTTENHILL

The Primitive Methodists had a Society in 1838 with 4 people on trial. There followed a blank period until 15 people were recorded in 1842. Numbers fluctuated from a low of 10 to a high of 39. Preaching was in Mr Belding's cottage c.1865. In 1873, it was agreed to accept Mrs Panton's offer for a preaching room in Tottenhill at £1 per year. A Chapel was built in 1881 for £156.

Sunday School started in 1874 with 7 teachers and 50 scholars. In 1900 there were 3 teachers and 20 scholars.

Society Stewards 1879-1900 included:- M Rylett, W Warren, W Lemon, Mrs Pitcher.

WORMEGAY

The Primitive Methodists had a Society in 1839 and over the next nine years membership varied from 9 to 30. Five roods of land were bought from Mr Lockwood at 4/- per yard in 1861. A Chapel was built in 1862 for £226. The Circuit Committee agreed that the roof be slated, the floors boarded and that the walls measure 14 feet to the wall board. The Wormegay trustees of the intended Chapel did not see 'eye to eye' with the Lynn Circuit Committee and there were arguments, over enfranchising the land, and the action of the trustees who had purchased materials, such as slates and bricks, before getting builders to tender. Fortunately, these obstacles were overcome.

Sunday School. In 1865 there were 12 teachers and 44 scholars. A schoolroom was built by Mr Baxter in 1867. Mr Brown was given permission to commence a day school in 1868. He was required to sign a stamped agreement that he would comply with the rules and conditions. In 1871 there were 8 teachers and 80 scholars, and in 1890,

11 teachers and 46 scholars. The Secretary in 1898 was J Harrod.

Temperance. In 1900, there were 21 juvenile and 5 adult abstainers.

Society Stewards 1897-1900:- C King, P Bowden.

A new Chapel was planned in 1881 and the Wormegay Society were advised to build using red and white bricks.

Marham notes:-
(1)The 1878 trust members were:- E Hewing, H Codling, G Nevelle, J Able, J Wilkinson, J Blanchflower, R Robutom, A Prater, G Baldry, N Baldry, W Dawe and N Holding.

Wereham notes:-
(1)Trustees in 1893 were:- Frederick Lambert labourer, John Lavender Local Preacher and farmer, Edward English labourer, Charles Pilgrim labourer and Class Leader, John Able Local Preacher and butcher, Samuel James Dane Local Preacher and bricklayer, Edward Thompson Local Preacher and gardener, Samuel Hall labourer, Harry Parker labourer.

Runcton Holme notes:-
(1)Trustees were:- Robert Williams, Henry Webb, James Pearson ? Boldero, Thomas Bowden senr, Thomas Bowden junr, William Seaman and James Gunton.
(2)Trustees in 1898 were:- Henry C Able of Magdalen, butcher; Thos W Huddlestone, Lynn, bootmaker; Walter Warren, Holme farmer; Charles Randall, Watlington, gardener; Jeremiah Wilkinson, Marham, baker; Chas F Wood, Fincham, baker.

Chapter twenty-nine

OTHER SOCIETIES PRE 1930

WOLFERTON

The Primitive Methodists had a small Society of 6 members plus 2 on trial in 1838. Services were held near the railway station in Mrs Claxton's cottage, on forms purchased by the Society. Up till 1848, numbers varied from 5 to 40. The leader was Abraham Claxton, a shoemaker. He was Society Steward from 1879-1889. Brother Gent was appointed leader in 1895. Efforts were made either to get a piece of land to build a Chapel, or to obtain a preaching room. The Circuit Authorities reluctantly decided on 2nd September 1907, *"that as no service has been held at Wolferton for a number of years, and that as there appears to be no probability of services being commenced there, that the name be removed from the plan."*

Abraham Claxton

STOKE FERRY

The Wesleyan Methodists had a Society with a Chapel of 258 seats, in the Downham Market Circuit.

The Primitive Methodists. In 1868, a schoolroom was hired for a rent, *"not to exceed £4 a year."* In 1869, Stoke Ferry came on the plan. The Authorities searched for land and considered buying the redundant Stoke Reform Chapel. However, an offer of a house for preaching was accepted. In 1876, the Authorities were still looking for land for a Chapel. R Reeson was Society Steward in 1879. Stoke Ferry was off the 1900 plan and was transferred to Downham Market Circuit.

BARTON

The Wesleyan Methodists had a 60 seat Chapel in 1873.

The Primitive Methodists had 10 members in 1842. Membership varied between 9 and 13 over the next seven years. A Chapel was enquired about in 1851. The Society received permission to raise a new class in 1859. Services were held in John Pealing's cottage c.1865.

The Society Steward in 1879 was J Lyndoe.

EAST MOOR (also known as 'Barton Eastmoor'.

The Primitive Methodist services recommenced there in 1884, when the Society Steward was W Lyndoe.

HOLLOW END

The Wesleyan Methodists had a Chapel, which Rev. Gunns (a PM Minister) was asked to hire in 1872, for a Missionary Meeting.

The Primitive Methodists earliest available record was September 1844, when anniversary services were planned on the first Sunday in April, to be preached by J Panton. Brother Flood was an Exhorter. Services were held in J Read's cottage c. 1865.

Sunday School. In 1846 there were 4 teachers and 22 scholars.

TOWER END

The Primitive Methodists held services in Patrick Shawl's house c.1865. In 1867 it was minuted, *"that the preachers planned at Tower End be required to preach in the open air."*

BROW 'O THE HILL

The Primitive Methodists had a Society in 1844/45. Thomas Mann was

Assistant Leader in 1868, with Brothers Pointer and Thompson. In October 1872, Brother Pointer of Ashwicken was asked, *"to take Brow of the Hill next Sunday and that he be asked to report to the committee what is the state of house and prospect for the society there."*

LEZIATE

The Wesleyan Methodists had a Society in 1837 with 7 people. By 1843 this had grown to 11.

The Primitive Methodists came on the plan in 1920. There were 4 people in the Society in 1924 and 2 from 1926 to 1929. Brother Wilkinson was Society Steward in 1923 and J Beckett in 1925. W Brewster was an Exhorter in 1926.

CASTLE RISING

The Primitive Methodists had a Society in 1866 when 5 people were on trial. Brother Smith of Wootton was leader. Mrs Catton of Grimston was approached regarding a house for preaching. In 1867 there were 11 members. Two years later it was decided, *"that Castle Rising have no appointments,"* and Brother Lee had permission, *"to get a house for religious services, if possible."*

WEST BILNEY

The Primitive Methodists remissioned the village in 1875 and later reported, *"that there was a good Society there."* W Hunter was Society Steward in 1879. West Bilney was taken off the plan in 1884 because there was no place to preach in. It was reported that *"the congregation have joined at East Winch."*

TERRINGTON GREEN

The Primitive Methodists had a Society in 1844. Mrs Allen was appointed Leader and her husband the assistant in 1845 when there were 4 members. The name was taken off the plan in 1846.

TILNEY BUCK CHAPEL

The Primitive Methodists. In 1846, the Circuit Committee decreed, *"that Mr Howchin preach Tilney Buck Chapel anniversary August 23rd 1846."*

MIDDLETON

The Wesleyan Methodists had a Chapel c.1865, with 140 seats.

The Primitive Methodists agreed at a Circuit Meeting in 1881, *"that Bro R Berry have sanction to hire the cottage at Middleton and that there be a collection the first Sunday on the new plan towards the expenses of seats and that they have a tea meeting."*

SETCHEY (SETCH)

The Wesleyan Methodists had a Society of one person in 1838/1839, and five in 1840.

The Primitive Methodists had a Society of three in 1842 and five in 1843. There is no further information.

CONGHAM

The Wesleyan Methodists had a Society of ten members recorded in 1841/1843. There is no further information.

TILNEY HIGH END

The Primitive Methodists had Six members in 1845. Brother Eggett was the Leader. The membership rose to ten, then dropped to four in 1848. Tilney High End returned on the plan in December 1869, and went off the plan in March 1870.

NORTH RUNCTON

The Wesleyan Methodists had a Society in 1837 with 16 members. Membership rose to 17 then fell back to 14 in 1843.

Chapter thirty

CLOSING THE CIRCLE

John Wesley died in 1791 having remained an Anglican Minister during his life. Four years later the Methodists were to separate from the Anglican Church. The Methodists were to suffer several schisms, as various factions left the main party to seek spiritual salvation under their own rules.

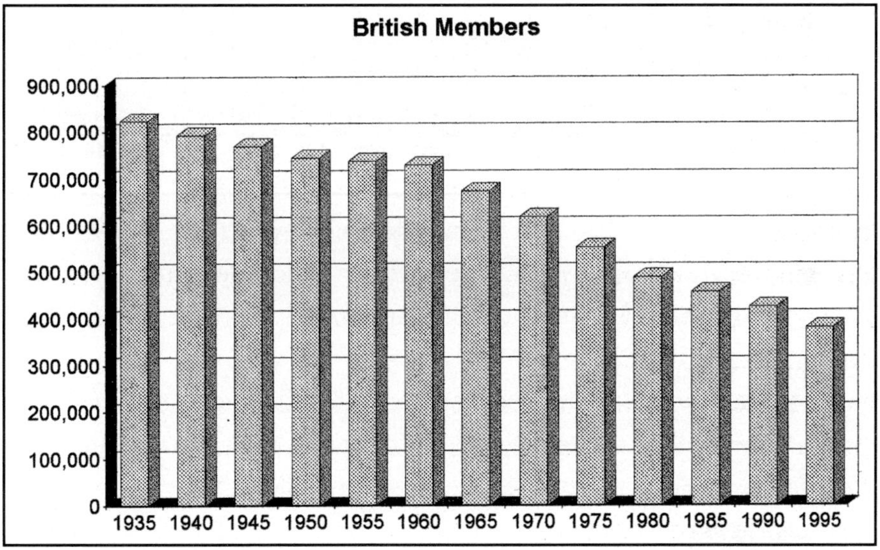

There was unity in 1932 when the Methodist Church was formed. Over the next sixty four years there has been a gradual decline in membership throughout Great Britain and the King's Lynn Circuit has suffered a similar rate of decline (see graph above and next page).

What of the next sixty years? It is possible that if the rate of decline continues, only a few Societies will survive. However, the underlying

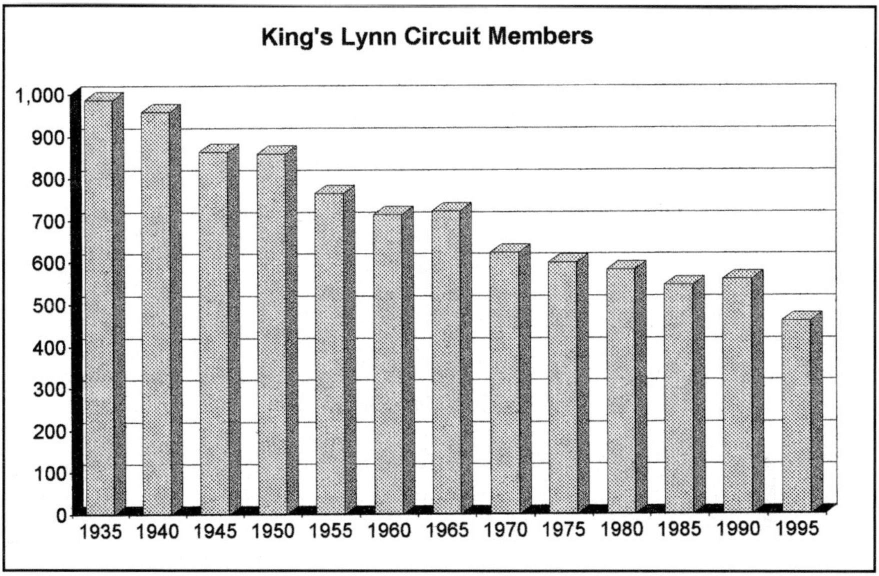

message is not all gloom and doom. At least three of the Societies are planning refurbishment, for example, major renovation and alterations at London Road, additions at Clenchwarton and improvements at West Lynn.

There is also the prospect of reunion with the Anglican Church, the Synod of whom has already agreed to unity talks. The Methodist Conference in June 1998 will actively debate the issue. There will be some issues to resolve and some areas to which each Church will wish to retain their own distinct identity; but the talks may bring everyone closer together and enable each Church to share resources whenever possible. The Reverend Colin Harbach, Superintendent Minister, writing in the November 1997 Clenchwarton Parish News, said "if we are truly Christian we are united to every other Christian because we all share in the life of Christ."

What action would John Wesley advocate if he were alive today?

Appendix I

Primary Sources consulted:-

The Journals of John Wesley.
Prim.Meth. Lynn Circuit Minute Books 1844-1922 (gaps 1850-57 and 1882-93).
PM Lynn Circuit Reports to District, 1846, 1849, 1853-1864, 1867.
PM Circuit Quarterday accounts Dec 1836-1848.
PM Circuit Stewards Accounts 1841-1859.
PM Lynn yearly reports of property 1922 and 1925-1932.
PM Lynn Circuit Schedules 1932.
PM Lynn Circuit Reports 1918-1921.
PM Connexion Report of the Sunday Schools 1874-1899.
PM Connexion Report of Lynn Station 1865-1900.
PM Schedule of the Sunday Schools 1917.
PM Circuit Plans; miscellaneous copies from 1844, with gaps from 1932.
Benevolent Society Charity Details 1806.
Smith's Charity details.
PM Lynn Circuit List of Members, 1838-1844.
The Consolidated General Minutes of the P.M. Connexion. 1870.
An Account of Chapels and Rooms (handwritten and unsigned) c.1865.
Terrington Minutes of the Burial Committee 1880.
Tower Street Leaders' Meetings 1915-1939.
Wesleyan Register of Members in the Lynn District 1882.
Wesleyan Circuit Schedule Book for Lynn 1837-1840.
Wesleyan Plans 1887, 1918, 1932.
Wesleyan Methodist Map 1873: Rev.E.H. Tindall.
Public Health Act. Preliminary Enquiry on the Borough of King's Lynn, 1853. H.M.S.O.
The Duties of Wesleyan Stewards: Edward Workman.
Hall's Circuits & Ministers 1765-1896.
Chapel Deeds, letters, posters, bills, etc.

Secondary Sources Consulted:-

Publication No.66: Wesley Historical Society, East Anglia Branch.
The Tale of the Years 1807-1907: E.A Harvey.
Primitive Methodism in King's Lynn Circuit 1821-1904: Rev.G Bell.1904.
A History of Primitive Methodism: W.G Gibbard.
Terrington St Clements Methodist Church Schoolroom Centenary 1885-1985: Rev.Robert A Richards B.A.
The History of King's Lynn: vol.2: Henry James Hillen. EP Publishing Ltd, A&C Black (Publishing) Ltd.
History of Lynn:Vol.2:William Richards M.A.1812.
Memories of Lynn:William Armes (papers read in 1858)Published in the Lynn Advertiser 1872.
The Lynn News & County Press, The Lynn Advertiser, The Lynn News & Advertiser.

Background Information:-

England in the Eighteenth Century (1714-1815): J.H Plumb.
England in the Twentieth Century: David Thomson.
English Social History: G.M Trevelyan.
History of England: Vol.2: T.B Macaulay.
A History of England: Keith Feiling.

Appendix I (continued)

The Church and the Age of Reason 1648-1789: G.R Cragg.
The English - A Social History 1066-1945: Christopher Hibbert.
The Idea of Poverty (England in the Early Industrial Age) Gertrude Himmelfarb.
The Village Labourer:J.L and Barbara Hammond.
The Skilled Labourer:J.L and Barbara Hammond.
Religion and Society in England, 1850-1914: Hugh McLeod.
John Wesley: Dr John Vickers.Methodist Publishing House.
John and Charles Wesley - The Preacher and the Poet : John Capon.
At Satan's Throne - The Story of Methodism in Bath. Ed. Bruce Crofts.
Victoria's Lynn. Boom & Prosperity: Vera Perrott.
Victoria's Lynn. Life & Leisure: Vera Perrott.
Halls of Zion (Chapels in Norfolk):Janet Ede, Norma Virgoe and Tom Williamson.
Stories of the Allen Family, West Lynn: Leslie Allen.
A Marshland Village: Terrington St. Clement History Group.

Appendix II

Ministers in the King's Lynn Circuit 1933-1996.

1933.	C.R Bower, E Marshall, C.G Oyston, C.J Clarke
1935.	E Marshall, A.J Ward, C.E.B Cowburn, C.J Clarke
1936.	E Marshall, A.J Ward, C.E.B Cowburn, H.G Rolls
1937.	A.J Ward, E.P Sellars, H.G Rolls, W.R Gilbert, Pastor J.V Staton
1938.	A.J Ward, E.P Sellars, H.G Rolls, W.R Gilbert, Pastor J.V Staton
1939.	A.J Ward, H.G Rolls, W.R Gilbert, J.E Thorp, Pastor W.E Bailey
1940.	H.A Stevens, H.G Rolls, C.G Balhatchet, J.E Thorp, R Lenton
1942.	H.A Stevens, H.G Rolls, C.G Balhatchet, F.W Loy, R Lenton
1943.	(W.H Armstrong), C.G Balhatchet, F.W Loy, W.E Paulson, R Lenton
1944.	(A Roughley), C.G Balhatchet, F.W Loy, W.E Paulson, W.H Robinson
1945	E.J Pike,W.E Paulson,W.H Robinson, W.H Middleton,Pastor A.A Groom
1946.	E.J Pike,G.B Middleton G.E Diggle,W.H Middleton, Pastor T.H Summers
1948.	T Featherstone, G.B Middleton, G.E Diggle, W.H Middleton
1950.	T Featherstone, R.L Hardwick, K.L Mowl, E Harrop
1951.	T Featherstone, F.L Henry, R.L Hardwick, K L Mowl
1952.	C McCarthy, F.L Henry, R.L Hardwick, K.L Mowl
1953.	C McCarthy, F.L Henry, C.E Dawes, H Bent
1956.	C McCarthy, C.E Dawes, H Bent, J.L Cooper
1957.	E Partner, J Garfoot, C.E Dawes, J.L Cooper
1958.	E Partner, J Garfoot, J.L Cooper, J.E Downes
1961.	E Partner, J Garfoot, D.M Caink, J.E Downes
1963.	H Lockwood, J Garfoot, D.M Caink, J.E Downes
1964.	H Lockwood, D.M Caink, J.E Downes, M Clark

Appendix II (continued)

1965.	H Lockwood, H.E Lacey, D.M Caink, M Clark
1967.	H Lockwood, G.L Hodson, H.E Lacey, M Clark
1969.	W.W.M White, G.L Hodson, A.R Bidnell, M Clark
1970.	W.W.M White, A.R Bidnell, H.A.J Smith
1973.	W.W.M White, A Windsor, H.A.J Smith
1974.	R Cullington, A Windsor, H.A.J Smith
1975.	R Cullington, A Windsor, F.E Sykes
1980.	W.H Mountford, A Windsor, F.E Sykes
1881.	W.H Mountford, A Windsor, R.A Richards
1982.	W.H Mountford, G.E Webster, R.A Richards
1985.	D.M Caink, G.E Webster, R.A Richards
1988.	D.M Caink, G.E Webster, D Blacklock
1989.	D.M Caink, C.B Holliday, D Blacklock.
1990.	A.I Hallworth, C.B Holliday, D Blacklock
1992.	C.B Holliday, C.D Harbach, D Blacklock
1993.	C.B Holliday, C.D Harback, B.P Savage
1994.	C.D Harbach, R.E Dolman, B.P Savage
1996.	C.D Harbach, R.E Dolman, B.P Savage.

Appendix III

Circuit Stewards in the Lynn Circuit 1933-1996.

1933.	N Clarke, G Alcock
1934.	N Clarke, B.W Jermyn
1935.	as 1934
1936.	as 1934
1937.	N Clarke, B.W Jermyn, W.H Barnes
1938.	W.H Barnes, N Clarke, C.K Butt
1939.	W.H Barnes, C.K Butt, C.W Lemon
1940.	W.H Barnes, C.K Butt, B.W Jermyn
1941.	as 1940
1942.	W.H Barnes, B.W Jermyn, L.W.A Barrett
1943.	W.H Barnes, H.R Croot, L.W.A Barrett
1944.	H.R Croot, C.J Young, B.W Jermyn
1945.	A.W Freeman, C.J Young, L.W.A Barrett.
1946.	as 1945
1947.	A.W Freeman, E Sketcher, L.W.A Barrett
1948.	as 1947
1949.	E Sketcher, L.W.A Barrett, S.F.V Bennett
1950.	L.W.A Barrett, S.F.V Bennett, G.F Rix
1951.	as 1950.

Appendix III (continued)

1952.	G.F Rix, L.W.A Barrett, K.J Curtis
1953.	G.F Rix, K.J Curtis, W.S.F Lane
1954.	K.J Curtis, W.S.F Lane, R.H Allen
1955.	as 1954
1956.	W.S.F Lane, R.H Allen, N Robinson
1957.	N Robinson, G.F. Merrywest, E.W.A Lloyd
1958.	as 1957
1959.	as 1957
1960.	as 1957
1961.	G.F Merrywest, E.W.A Lloyd
1962.	as 1961.
1963.	as 1961
1964.	E.W.A Lloyd, A Boyce, H Goodley
1965.	as 1964
1966.	H Goodley, A Boyce, A.J Goble
1967.	R.J Charlesworth, E.H Garfoot
1968.	as 1967
1969.	as 1967
1970.	R.J Charlesworth, V Price-Jones
1971.	R.J Charlesworth, V Price-Jones, E.H Garfoot
1972.	as 1971
1973.	R.J Charlesworth, V Price-Jones, G Cornthwaite
1974.	V Price-Jones, G Cornthwaite
1975.	as 1974
1976.	as 1974
1977.	G Cornthwaite, P Gaskin (6 months), M Havery
1978.	G Cornthwaite, M Havery
1979	as 1978
1980.	as 1978
1981.	M Havery, R Hamon, Mrs B Smith
1982.	as 1981
1983.	as 1981
1984.	as 1981
1985.	R Hamon, Mrs B Smith, J Deas
1986.	as 1985
1987.	Mrs B Smith, J Deas, J Woodcock
1988.	as 1987
1989.	J Deas, J Woodcock, G Uttin
1990.	as 1989
1991.	J Woodcock, G Uttin, J Shaw
1992.	as 1991
1993.	J Woodcock (to September), G Uttin, J Shaw, Mrs J Hamon
1994.	G Uttin, Mrs J Hamon
1995.	as 1994
1996.	G Uttin, Mrs J Hamon, J Stent (Oct-Dec).